THE BEDFORD SERIES IN HISTORY AND CULTURE

England's Glorious Revolution, 1688–1689

A Brief History with Documents

Related Titles in
THE BEDFORD SERIES IN HISTORY AND CULTURE
Advisory Editors: Lynn Hunt, *University of California, Los Angeles*
David W. Blight, *Yale University*
Bonnie G. Smith, *Rutgers University*
Natalie Zemon Davis, *Princeton University*
Ernest R. May, *Harvard University*

THE BEDFORD SERIES IN HISTORY AND CULTURE

England's Glorious Revolution,

1688–1689

A Brief History with Documents

Steven C. A. Pincus

Yale University

BEDFORD/ST. MARTIN'S   Boston ♦ New York

For Bedford/St. Martin's
Executive Editor for History: Mary V. Dougherty
Director of Development for History: Jane Knetzger
Senior Developmental Editor: Heidi L. Hood
Editorial Assistants: Rachel Safer, Shannon Hunt
Senior Production Supervisor: Joe Ford
Production Associate: Christopher Gross
Senior Marketing Manager: Jenna Bookin Barry
Project Management: Books By Design, Inc.
Indexer: Books By Design, Inc.
Text Design: Claire Seng-Niemoeller
Cover Design: Billy Boardman
Cover Art: William of Orange (William III of England) and Queen Mary. Engraving, 1689. Snark/Art Resource, N.Y.
Composition: Stratford Publishing Services, Inc.
Printing and Binding: RR Donnelley & Sons Company

President: Joan E. Feinberg
Editorial Director: Denise B. Wydra
Director of Marketing: Karen Melton Soeltz
Director of Editing, Design, and Production: Marcia Cohen
Manager, Publishing Services: Emily Berleth

Library of Congress Control Number: 2005924208

Manufactured in the United States of America.

For information, write: Bedford/St. Martin's, 75 Arlington Street, Boston, MA 02116 (617-399-4000)

ISBN-10: 0-312-16714-8 (paperback)
          1-4039-7154-4 (hardcover)
ISBN-13: 978-0-312-16714-1 (paperback)
          978-1-4039-7154-8 (hardcover)

Acknowledgment

Document 21: From John Evelyn, *Diary of John Evelyn,* E. S. De Beer, ed. (Oxford: Clarendon Press, 1955), vol. 4, 331, 380. By permission of Oxford University Press.

Foreword

The Bedford Series in History and Culture is designed so that readers can study the past as historians do.

The historian's first task is finding the evidence. Documents, letters, memoirs, interviews, pictures, movies, novels, or poems can provide facts and clues. Then the historian questions and compares the sources. There is more to do than in a courtroom, for hearsay evidence is welcome, and the historian is usually looking for answers beyond act and motive. Different views of an event may be as important as a single verdict. How a story is told may yield as much information as what it says.

Along the way the historian seeks help from other historians and perhaps from specialists in other disciplines. Finally, it is time to write, to decide on an interpretation and how to arrange the evidence for readers.

Each book in this series contains an important historical document or group of documents, each document a witness from the past and open to interpretation in different ways. The documents are combined with some element of historical narrative—an introduction or a biographical essay, for example—that provides students with an analysis of the primary source material and important background information about the world in which it was produced.

Each book in the series focuses on a specific topic within a specific historical period. Each provides a basis for lively thought and discussion about several aspects of the topic and the historian's role. Each is short enough (and inexpensive enough) to be a reasonable one-week assignment in a college course. Whether as classroom or personal reading, each book in the series provides firsthand experience of the challenge—and fun—of discovering, recreating, and interpreting the past.

Lynn Hunt
David W. Blight
Bonnie G. Smith
Natalie Zemon Davis
Ernest R. May

Preface

The Revolution of 1688–89 in England was the first modern social and political revolution to transform the Early Modern European world. It made possible the industrial revolution of the late eighteenth and nineteenth centuries. It provided a model explicitly for revolutionaries in both North America and France, as these revolutionaries acknowledged. Yet until now, no materials were readily available for classroom use that make the significance and excitement of the event accessible to students. Two factors explain this gap. First, while eighteenth-century Europeans and Americans were almost unanimous in their admiration for the transformations wrought in England in the late 1680s and 1690s, most twentieth-century historians have followed Edmund Burke in denying that the Revolution of 1688–89 bore any resemblance to the French Revolution. Second, until recently, most of the key documents necessary to understand the Revolution of 1688–89 were available only in manuscript or the rare books rooms of a very few libraries. This volume makes key documents readily available and will therefore enable students and instructors to explore and debate the idea that the "Glorious Revolution" should be considered the first modern revolution.

The introduction in Part One, "The Revolution of 1688–1689: The First Modern Revolution," provides a comprehensive guide to understanding the Revolution of 1688–89. It lays out the dramatic story of William of Orange's arrival in England and the collapse of James II's regime in November and December 1688. It then introduces students to the contours of the interpretive debate about the revolution that began in the late eighteenth century. Whereas most accounts of the revolution focus exclusively on the high politics and religious developments of 1688–89, the introduction to this volume encourages students to widen their fields of vision. It sets the revolution firmly in its social as well as its political context, and lays out the political consequences of the revolution more broadly. It asks students to think beyond the British to the European and extra-European consequences of the revolution. They are prompted to think about not only the constitutional results of the revolution, but also the resulting changes in social and economic policy. In so doing, it is hoped, students will come to appreciate the revolution from multiple perspectives—from the perspective of the politician as well as from the person on the street, and from the perspective of London as well as from Paris and Amsterdam. Finally, to bring the significance of the ideological struggle of 1688–89 into sharper relief, students are asked to consider the ideas of two of the most widely read political writers of the late seventeenth century: Roger L'Estrange and John Locke, the first a fervent defender of James II's regime, the second a revolutionary who later served in William III's government.

The documents in Part Two are organized to parallel the explanation laid out in the introduction. Taken from both manuscripts and printed sources, the documents illustrate both the social and the political context of the revolution and give a sense of the arguments advanced by James II's supporters and detractors. They also address issues of foreign policy, political economy, and religion. Chosen to provoke the best discussion and the most intense engagement from students, the documents range from excerpts of sermons to policy memoranda, eyewitness accounts of events, legal pronouncements, and selections from the works of Roger L'Estrange and John Locke. Taken together, the documents offer readers a solid foundation for understanding the significance of the revolution from the perspective of those who lived through it. Whereas modern accounts of the Revolution of 1688–89 are colored by the knowledge that England did not have a nineteenth-century revolution, this collection provides a corrective through the accounts of those who saw England as a politically and socially volatile place.

The texts and commentary in this volume were assembled with several different classroom uses in mind. This book could be easily incorporated in a survey of Early Modern British history as well as a Western or European Civilization course. Because different instructors in these courses will want to emphasize different themes, this book includes a variety of materials on society, religion, political economy, popular politics, foreign policy, and the constitution. This book is also designed for instructors teaching surveys of political thought or intellectual history. Because teachers of Locke's *Two Treatises* or his *Letter on Toleration* often find it challenging to explain to students what was exercising Locke, this collection places Locke's writings, which are central to understanding the revolution, for the first time in their broader socioeconomic and political context. The other advantage of this collection is that it places Locke alongside one of his chief contemporary polemical adversaries, Roger L'Estrange, for the first time.

To further aid students, the appendixes include a chronology of English political history in the later seventeenth century, a series of questions for consideration to prompt students to think broadly about the dramatic events of the revolution, and a selected bibliography to frame student assignments.

A NOTE ABOUT THE TEXT

As I began working on a monograph on England's Revolution of 1688–89, I became increasingly aware that scholars based their accounts on a relatively small set of sources that explored a well-defined set of issues. Yet, in my own research I was finding that contemporaries of the English Revolution were discussing a broader set of issues. This collection aims to introduce students both to the types of materials that scholars have traditionally used and to new documents that have rarely played a part in the story of the revolution. To make these documents more accessible, I have modernized spelling and punctuation throughout. I also chose select passages from the documents to make their relationship with each other and with the revolution readily apparent. As a result, I hope both students and their teachers will find it easier to place the ideas of the many observers of the revolution in historical context.

ACKNOWLEDGMENTS

This volume could not have been produced without the help of a number of individuals. Ryan Frace, Brent Sirota, Abby Swingen, and Jessica Hanser all played vital roles in identifying and transcribing the documents in the collection. Abby Swingen and Brent Sirota have been invaluable in helping me to piece together the various parts of this project. I am also indebted to my students at the University of Chicago, who have served as sounding board for a number of the texts reproduced in this collection as well as for the arguments advanced in the introduction.

At Bedford/St. Martin's, Senior Developmental Editor Heidi Hood and Editorial Assistants Rachel Safer and Shannon Hunt played a vital role in bringing this volume through the press. I also wish to acknowledge Executive Editor Mary Dougherty, Director of Development for History Jane Knetzger, and Manager of Publishing Services Emily Berleth for their efforts.

I have also benefited from the comments of the reviewers for the press: Jeffrey Auerbach, California State University, Northridge; Alastair Bellany, Rutgers University–New Brunswick; David Cressy, The Ohio State University; Carol Englehardt, Wright State University; Amy Thompson McCandless, College of Charleston; Molly McClain, University of San Diego; Ethan Shagan, Northwestern University; Laura Smoller, University of Arkansas, Little Rock; Stephen Joseph Sitwell Jr., University of Texas at Arlington; and Rachel Weil, Cornell University. Rachel Weil has been particularly helpful in discussing in depth some ideas for revision.

I am also grateful to my wife, Sue Stokes, for reading everything and being unfailingly supportive. Sam, too, had to hear much of this presented to his seventh grade class at Chicago's Lab School, and had the good grace to say that it was interesting. Little David made sure that the last set of revisions were conducted with little sleep but much good cheer.

Steven C. A. Pincus

Contents

England's Glorious Revolution, 1688–1689

A Brief History with Documents

PART ONE

Introduction

The Revolution of 1688–1689:
The First Modern Revolution

On November 5, 1688, after months of preparation and one false start, William Prince of Orange arrived at Torbay on England's southwestern coast with an army perhaps as large as twenty-one thousand men. On its face, the invasion seemed doomed to disaster. Exactly one hundred years earlier, the Spanish, then the greatest power in Western Europe, had attempted to invade England with a huge army and an incomparable fleet. England's Queen Elizabeth (r. 1558–1603) had no military experience and, what was worse, a makeshift navy and no regular army. Nevertheless, the Spanish armada never landed in England, having been defeated in battle by the English and dispersed by the unpredictable and stormy weather of the North Sea. Later, in the summer of 1685, just prior to William's sailing, the illegitimate son of Charles II (r. 1660–85), James Duke of Monmouth, had led an invasion of England from the Dutch Republic. He landed in the west of England at Lyme Regis, not too far from Torbay. Yet within a matter of weeks, Monmouth's attempt to seize the crown from his uncle, James II (r. 1685–88), in 1685 had met with utter and complete defeat. Monmouth himself was beheaded, and his followers were rounded up and either executed or transported as servants to English possessions in North America.

Prince William's initial reception in England's West Country must have filled him with a sense of foreboding. William, who was the Dutch stadtholder (the military but not political leader of the Dutch Republic) and an experienced soldier, was not initially welcomed with wild cheering and celebrating maidens as his ill-fated cousin, Monmouth, had been three years before. Instead, William was initially met with reticence, caution, and reserve. The inhabitants of the West Country were wary of supporting yet another failed invasion. However, William soon had reason to shed his habitual formality and shyness. Common people, gentry, and nobility, disgusted with James II's government but fearing his power, soon found the courage to pour into William's camp and rise independently throughout England, offering both physical and financial support. After the revolutionaries gained local control, in town squares and coffeehouses throughout the kingdom they read aloud William's *Declaration* (see Document 2), which announced his reasons for intervening in English politics. Each reading of the *Declaration,* it seemed, was followed by another round of toasts to the success of William, England's new hero and deliverer. Simultaneously, noblemen, substantial gentry, and more humble townspeople throughout the kingdom—most of whom had long known of William's plans and many of whom had invited him to England—rose in support of the Dutch prince who was also the husband of James II's own daughter Mary. These giddy rebels were England's "desperate thousands," as the Williamite supporter Colley Cibber described them—desperate because, should William fail, they would be judged guilty of treason (see Document 5).

Although William was successful in the end, he had some disadvantages. Unlike Queen Elizabeth in 1588, James had a huge professional army at his disposal. This army was well versed and drilled in all the methods of modern warfare. It was, observed two well-informed London merchants, "the completest army, perhaps, in the world" (Document 3). Yet as William, his troops, and his new crew of enthusiastic volunteers marched on James II's army, the English king lost his nerve. Some of James II's officer corps, the pride and joy of his kingdom, deserted to the invading force. John Churchill,[1] James II's lifelong friend and the lieutenant general of the army, was only one of the most devastating deserters. He was joined by men like the Duke of

---

[1]John Churchill, Lord Marlborough (1650–1722), a longtime friend and confidant of James II; made 1st Earl of Marlborough (1689), 1st Duke of Marlborough (1702), and commander in chief of the armed forces under both William III and Anne I (1701–1711).

Grafton, James II's nephew, and the Duke of Ormond and Lord Cornbury, both of whose families had long and loyally served the Stuart royal family. Princess Anne, James II's own younger daughter, had fled to join William's supporters in Nottingham. Mobs throughout the kingdom rose against their governors. Townspeople threw out military governors. Rural laborers attacked the houses and lands of James II's greatest supporters in Kent, Lancashire, Yorkshire, and the West Country. Hearing all this news, James II retreated from Salisbury to London and placed his fleeting hopes on a negotiated settlement. Instead of having to fight his way to London, William was escorted the entire way by cheering crowds.

James II fled to France on December 23, 1688, less than two months after William of Orange arrived in England. It had become clear to James that a negotiated settlement would strip him of all his power. Persistent mob violence in London and throughout the country convinced him that nothing could protect his person or his family. Then, between January 22 and August 20, 1689, a Parliament made up of England's substantial gentlemen and noblemen met and declared William and his wife, Mary—who as James II's eldest daughter had a strong hereditary claim to the throne—king and queen. At every stage in their deliberations, the House of Commons and the House of Lords were encouraged by thousands of men and women assembled outside their chambers. England had new rulers who, it appeared, were placed on the throne by the will of the English people. The power of that throne, Parliament implied in its Declaration of Rights, was limited by the rights of English subjects (see Document 12).

The new monarchs soon reversed many of the policies of the old regime. Whereas James II had admired France's great monarch, Louis XIV, William and Mary declared war against France. Whereas James II promoted an imperial policy based on the ideas and aspirations of the East India Company, William and Mary turned against that company and preferred instead to support the development of England's fledgling manufacturing industries. Whereas Charles II and his younger brother, James II, had promoted clerics within the Church of England who celebrated the divine right of kings and the necessity for a compulsory, uniform state church, William and Mary promoted new bishops who advocated religious toleration and insisted on the limited nature of royal authority. On May 24, 1689, Parliament passed the Act of Toleration, guaranteeing freedom of worship for all Protestants. William and Mary personally protected the right to worship of most other religious minorities (see Document 36).

Participants and observers were unanimous in declaring England's transformation revolutionary. "I question if in all the histories of empire there is one instance of so bloodless a revolution as that in England in 1688," gushed the revolutionary volunteer Colley Cibber. He reflected incredulously that a nation so recently riven by violent party squabbles—indeed, the political parties of Whig and Tory had been born merely ten years before over the possible accession of James II to the crown[2]—could unite so quickly and so universally. As Cibber noted, 1688 was a time when "Whigs, Tories, princes, prelates, nobles, clergy, common people, and a standing army, were unanimous. To have seen all England of one mind is to have lived at a very particular juncture. Happy nation . . . !" (Document 5). The London merchants Francis Barrington and Benjamin Steele, who were compelled to give up trading in the tumultuous months of the revolution, were equally impressed. "Now certainly when the providences of God are considered in this whole transaction," they explained to their Tunis-based trading partners, "never anything happened with so many amazing circumstances as this hath done—the bonding of the spirits of people so universally one way, nay even the minds of persons whose long differings with each other made one think 'twas impossible they should be reconciled in anything, did all agree to help on this work; the speediness of its execution; and all without the loss of 50 men on all sides—makes it the most astonishing alteration that ever yet befell any one part of the universe" (Document 3).

By all contemporary accounts, the revolution was a wondrous one. Indeed, as early as December 1688, observers called it the "Glorious Revolution." The term originally referred to the improbability of the event and the rapidity with which James II was overthrown. Over time, scholars have used the term *Glorious Revolution* to differentiate the Revolution of 1688–89 from subsequent great revolutions. *Glorious* came to mean bloodless and hence conservative. However, because the revolution effected changes more radical than previously supposed, it is more accurate to refer to this series of events instead as the "Revolution of 1688–89."

[2]The Tory Party was created in 1679 to 1681 in opposition to the Whigs. Where the Whigs hoped to exclude James Duke of York from the throne, the Tories wanted to ensure that he would eventually be crowned James II. Through the cut and thrust of debate in that political crisis, Whigs came to be associated with policies of religious toleration and political resistance. Tories came to be associated with religious uniformity and unconditional political loyalty or passive obedience.

Before the revolution itself was over, fierce debates began about the causes and consequences of the event. This debate raged from the 1690s through the end of the eighteenth century. In 1789, on the one hundred and first anniversary of William of Orange's landing in England, the most celebrated English Dissenting cleric of the eighteenth century and a prominent supporter of the American Revolution, Richard Price, stood up to address his fellow members of the Revolution Society at the meetinghouse in the Old Jewry just outside London's Guildhall. In his sermon, *A Discourse on the Love of Our Country*, which in print instantly became a best-seller in Britain and throughout Europe, Price admonished his audience to revere the principles of 1688–89. "By a bloodless victory, the fetters which despotism had been long preparing for us were broken," Price recalled. "The rights of the people were asserted, a tyrant expelled, and a sovereign of our own choice appointed in his room. Security was given to our property, and our consciences were emancipated. The bounds of free enquiry were enlarged." In short, Price argued, the "era of light and liberty was introduced among us, by which we have been made an example to other kingdoms, and became the instructors of the world" (Document 6).

Price's optimistic, open-ended, and radical commentary on the meaning of the Revolution of 1688–89 elicited a number of critical responses. But no response to Richard Price's *Discourse* was more famous, more influential, or more widely read than that of Edmund Burke. Burke felt compelled to write his *Reflections on the Revolution in France* (1790) to dispel the dangerous principles espoused by Dr. Price. Burke duly recorded "the dislike I feel to revolutions, the signals which have so often been given from pulpits" — reminding his readers that Price had celebrated the principles of 1688–89 from the pulpit of the Dissenting meetinghouse in the Old Jewry. Burke, like his antagonist Price, found much to celebrate in 1688–89. But unlike Price, Burke argued that there had been no innovation, no revolution, but merely a sensible and backward-looking restoration of the old order. The Revolution of 1688–89 was motivated by not a single new idea. James II had been the radical revolutionary; the English people had merely restored normalcy in 1688–89. "The Revolution was made to preserve our ancient indisputable laws and liberties, and that ancient constitution of government which is our only security for law and liberty," Burke explained. "The very idea of the fabrication of a new government, is enough to fill us with disgust and horror. We wished at the period of the Revolution, and do now wish, to derive all we possess as an inheritance from our forefathers" (Document 7). Price had deemed the Revolution of 1688–89 worthy of celebration and commemoration because it so dramatically transformed, and transformed for the better in his view, England's political and social orientation. For Burke, by contrast, the glory of the Revolution of 1688–89 was precisely that it changed so little, that it restored the English ancient constitution that had been threatened by a Catholic tyrant, with a minimum of constitutional and social disruption.

Burke's conclusion that England had an unrevolutionary revolution has been adopted in modified form by almost all later commentators. Scholars now generally agree that England's Revolution of 1688–89 was a sensible and not a radical corrective for a kingdom derailed by an ambitious Catholic king. There is a general consensus that England had a narrowly political revolution in 1688–89 that prevented it from having a more modern social revolution at a later date. Some scholars have emphasized the extent to which England's political elites wanted to reverse James II's reliance on unusual, and largely Roman Catholic, political advisers. For these scholars, 1688–89 was about restoring the old political order. Others have insisted that the English Protestant majority wanted to reverse their Catholic king's preferential treatment for his co-religionists. These historians understand the revolution as a war of religion. All agree, however, that it was a largely bloodless event that restored England's ancient polity and England's Protestant religion. England's Revolution of 1688–89 was restorative not innovative, conservative not radical.[3]

The claim that England had an unrevolutionary revolution is necessarily a comparative one. The Revolution of 1688–89, in this view, was simply not as revolutionary as the French, American, Russian, or Mexican revolutions. These modern revolutions, scholars insist, changed not only the political actors, but also the socioeconomic, moral, and cultural outlooks of their regimes. Unlike the Revolution of 1688–89, modern revolutions aim to create a new world, not restore an old one, they say. The framework for the comparison is, however, deeply

---

[3]There is one prominent and significant exception to this rule. Professor Jonathan Israel has argued that the Revolution of 1688–89 did radically transform English, and indeed European, politics. For Israel, this was the intended consequence of the revolution. However, he argues that this radicalism derives from the fact that England was conquered by William's Dutch army. As a result, William imposed a new set of political ideas on the English nation. The documents provided below should allow one to assess whether the values and policies adopted after the revolution were indigenous ones or imposed from outside.

flawed. Scholars of these revolutions insist that it took well over a decade for the revolutionary impulses to play themselves out.[4] Students of the Revolution of 1688–89, taking their cue from Edmund Burke, have instead focused narrowly on the years of James II's regime and the months following his fall from power. The French revolutionary decades are compared with the months of June 1688 to February 1689 in England. British historians have traditionally asked why James II was forced to leave England in December 1688 with hardly a shot having been fired. Why was the Revolution of 1688–89 bloodless?

By altering the traditional chronological framework, documents collected in this volume elicit a different set of questions leading to new conclusions. Why was James II's regime replaced with the regime of William and Mary? Did these two regimes pursue different agendas? Were they committed to different political ideologies? Did the Revolution of 1688–89 reorient England's social and economic policies? If so, were these differences revolutionary?

ENGLISH ECONOMY AND SOCIETY IN 1685

Most accounts of revolutions begin with depictions of a rapidly changing social and economic system: This is because revolutions are rightly described as the consequences of processes of modernization. The possibility of material improvement makes it possible for most people to imagine social and political arrangements better than those enjoyed by their ancestors. While most historians of the Revolution of 1688–89 have neglected the social and economic contexts of their story,[5] there can be no doubt that England in the seventeenth century had experienced rapid and pronounced change. England in the late seventeenth century acquired many of the attributes of a modern commercial society.

While England in the sixteenth century had been almost entirely an agricultural society, it had ceased to be so by the time of the revolution. Only about half of England's population was primarily involved

---

[4]For some well-known examples, see Francois Furet (trans. by Antonia Nevill), *The French Revolution, 1770–1814* (Oxford: Basil Blackwell, 1996); Sheila Fitzpatrick, *The Russian Revolution*, 2nd ed. (Oxford: Oxford University Press, 1994), 3–4; and Alan Knight, *The Mexican Revolution* (Cambridge: Cambridge University Press, 1986), vol. 2, 517–27.

[5]The great exception is Thomas Babington Macaulay's *History of England from the Accession of James II*. Macaulay's famous third chapter, in which he describes the condition of England in 1685, is often depicted as the founding moment of social history.

in agriculture in the late seventeenth century, a figure roughly comparable to the United States on the eve of the American Civil War. Although England had been an economic backwater in the sixteenth century, the Dutch Republic had emerged as Europe's prime manufacturer in the late seventeenth century. The evidence suggests that much of England's transformation from an agrarian to a manufacturing society occurred in the second half of the seventeenth century.

By the late seventeenth century, the English produced a wide range of manufactured goods. Cloth making was England's leading industry, as it had been for centuries. But over the course of the seventeenth century, English cloth producers significantly retooled and shifted the focus of their manufacturing. Previously, the English had produced heavy woolen broadcloths appropriate for the colder climates of Northern Europe. By the accession of James II, English manufacturers produced new, lighter cloths involving mixes of wool and linen that were appropriate for the warmer climates of Southern Europe and the New World. In fact, woolen goods had ceased to be the only manufactured products exported from England. A wide range of English products replaced imports on the English market and began to compete successfully abroad. Sugar refineries, glass makers, pottery makers, and iron foundries proliferated in the late seventeenth century. English shipbuilding grew more rapidly in the seventeenth century than anytime before or since. After 1600, English miners produced much more coal, tin, iron ore, and lead than ever before. By the 1680s, England had become a nation of manufacturers.

Not only did England become a more commercial society over the course of the seventeenth century, it became a more urban society. The percentage of English people living in urban environments rose dramatically. Whereas between 10 and 12 percent of English people lived in towns in the early sixteenth century, as many as 40 percent lived in urban areas by 1700. The United States did not achieve a comparable urbanization rate until after the Civil War. This rapid urbanization set England apart from all of continental Europe outside the Dutch Republic. Whereas most of Europe was becoming less urban in the late seventeenth century, England's towns enjoyed sustained growth.

Much, but not all, of England's urban growth was attributable to the remarkable growth of the capital, London. London grew from a population of 75,000 in 1550 to a population of 575,000 in 1700. In the reign of James II, London was the largest city in Europe. Many of the cities that would later become England's industrial centers also grew dramatically in the seventeenth century. Birmingham, Leeds, Manchester, Newcastle, Liverpool, Sheffield, and Portsmouth were all transformed from small villages to bustling cities. Philadelphia, New York, and Boston—none of which had existed at the beginning of the seventeenth century—were among the larger cities under English rule. Norwich, Exeter, and Bristol, already substantial places in 1600, grew considerably over the course of the seventeenth century.

Not only did England's towns grow dramatically in the seventeenth century, they also became more comfortable places to live. Houses became bigger and more sturdy. Mud walls and thatched roofs were replaced by brick and tile. Streets were widened and paved. Towns and cities, which had been universally dark at night, were now graced for the first time with public streetlights. The threat of fire, the bane of early modern urban dwellers, was diminished by the advent almost simultaneously of fire departments and fire insurance. As an increasingly large percentage of the population was paid with money rather than goods, shops, already present in larger market towns before the seventeenth century, proliferated. Urban dwellers could now visit cookshops, bookshops, barber shops, and purveyors of groceries in humble villages as well as in the urban metropolis (see Document 9).

Economic improvement and urban growth spawned a variety of new leisure options as well. From the 1650s, coffechouses spread throughout the country at a rapid pace (see Document 11). By the end of the century, there were said to be several thousand coffee-houses in London alone, but even modest towns like Kendal, Carlisle, and Preston in the northwest of England had their own popular coffee-houses. In 1661, London's first pleasure garden (early modern amusement park), the Vauxhall Gardens, opened on the south bank of the Thames. Urban amenities were supplemented by the emergence of leisure towns. Spas were all the rage in late-seventeenth-century England. The most famous and elite were at Bath and Tunbridge Wells, but similar if less elaborate resorts opened in Derbyshire, Yorkshire, and Berkshire and in the London suburb of Islington.

England's rapidly developing infrastructure facilitated the trends toward urbanization and commercialization. The passage of the first turnpike act in 1663 was a landmark in the development of England's network of roads. Soon stagecoaches, rarities before the 1640s, were offering regularly scheduled service to all of England's major towns and many minor ones. Wagons and carts plied the same routes with commercial merchandise. London had more than six hundred hackney coaches, which were essentially early modern taxis, to take passengers to their destinations. England's rivers were increasingly busy with passenger and commercial barges. An even greater amount of traffic traveled on the regular coastal routes, taking, for example, coal from Newcastle to London. The post office, which had only really carried court correspondence before the 1630s, became the primary institution of commercial and personal interchange in the late seventeenth century. The creation of the Penny Post in the late 1670s guaranteed same-day delivery of letters throughout the greater London area for a single penny. The rapidly expanding road system and the ever intensifying network of local post offices guaranteed slightly slower but no less regular delivery throughout England.

Increasing urbanization, combined with a rapidly intensifying infrastructure, made it possible for England to develop a remarkable news culture in the late seventeenth century. The English, it is true, already had a well-developed taste for news before the outbreak of the English Civil War in the 1640s. After the Civil War and the elimination of press censorship, however, newspapers, newsletters, and pamphlets debating the significance of recent events proliferated. From the 1650s, the new coffeehouses provided ideal sites for debate, discussion, and dissemination of the latest information. By the accession of James II, the English were known throughout Europe as a news-hungry people.

England in the late seventeenth century was developing many of the characteristics of a modern society. England's commerce was growing faster than its population. The country was increasingly urban. Local and regional economies were being integrated into a national economic system. Modern economic instruments—such as private banking, insurance, and paper money—were becoming common. And England was deviating from the European economic norm. Whereas the sixteenth and early seventeenth centuries had been boom years for most of Europe, only England and the Netherlands enjoyed sustained economic growth after the 1620s. In large part this was because England's extensive overseas trade with the East and West Indies and North America made it relatively immune to the increasing tide of economic protectionist barriers that swept through Europe at the time (see Documents 8–10). England could survive the exclusion of its manufactures from European markets in part because it could continue to export them to its colonies. It could survive without many European raw materials and luxury goods because it was agriculturally self-sufficient and because it could import sugar and tobacco from the New World and fabrics and spices from the East. England's position in the Atlantic world markets set it apart from its European economic competitors, allowing it to become one of the first modern economies.

Failure to recognize England's economic and social transformation in the late seventeenth century has deeply distorted the traditional interpretation of the Revolution of 1688–89. When the great nineteenth-century Whig historian Thomas Babington Macaulay concluded that the revolution was a deeply conservative event, he did so in large part because he believed that England's society in the late seventeenth century was hopelessly backward and that a backward society could not produce a modern revolution. But the mass of social and economic historians since Macaulay's time have demonstrated that far from being an economic backwater, England was a rapidly modernizing society in the late seventeenth century.

ENGLISH POLITICS IN 1685

England's political life in the mid- to late seventeenth century was similarly marked by great change. Because England in the seventeenth century was politically violent rather than politically stable, most Europeans thought of England as a remarkably tumultuous place. Between 1640 and 1660, the British Isles were torn apart by a series of civil wars. In January 1649, a parliamentary tribunal judged Charles I, the father of both Charles II and James II, guilty of treason and had him beheaded. The ensuing eleven-year interregnum dramatically transformed England's political and social landscape. The House of Lords was abolished. Parliament implemented land taxes on England's social elite for the first time. In the absence of a coercive state church (government by bishops was eliminated in October 1640), a bewildering variety of sects emerged. For many scholars in the nineteenth and twentieth centuries, this was *the* English revolution.

As great as the midcentury convulsion was, however, it was followed by the restoration of the monarchy in 1660. Charles II returned from his continental exile, along with his brother James, in triumph. After almost a decade of political upheaval that had intensified after the Protector Oliver Cromwell's death in 1658, the English people were ready for a return to traditional rule. Crowds enthusiastically cheered Charles II's arrival in London, hoping that the return of the king would bring with it the return of political stability. His first Parliament, elected in 1662, restored the power of the monarchy. Charles II quickly regained almost all of the executive powers his father had bargained away in the 1640s. The Act of Uniformity of 1662 once again made the Church of England the only legal religious body in England. English men and women were once again compelled by law to attend Church of England services on Sundays. The Civil War and the interregnum had turned England upside down, but the Restoration had almost turned it right back up again.

Almost, but not quite. Because of the high cost of fighting first civil wars and then foreign wars in the 1640s and 1650, the English state was forced to devise new forms of taxation and develop vast new layers of bureaucracy. As a result the English state was much more powerful in 1662 than it had been in 1640. England now had a professional army and navy, if somewhat reduced from their size in the 1650s. England now had a more extensive state infrastructure, supported by a larger network of roads than had existed before the Civil War. Charles II also had to contend with a much more deeply politicized nation. While the new king had been welcomed enthusiastically by a substantial portion of the nation, a much larger proportion of that nation had become consumers of political information in the tumultuous two decades since the outbreak of the Civil War and had become more critical and wary. While the Church of England reclaimed the legal religious monopoly, many in England had actively read and debated the variety of religious pamphlets, sermons, and broadsides easily available from the early 1640s. Religiously, politically, and economically, the English ruled by Charles II were a different people than his father had governed.

Tensions between Charles II's restored monarchy and his political and religious critics came to a head in the late 1670s. Three successive Parliaments raised profound questions about the nature and power of Charles II's regime. The crisis was set off by the twin fears of increasing French power on the continent and the realization that Charles II's brother and heir, James Duke of York, was a Roman Catholic. Charles II's critics, who came to be known as the Whig Party—named after the virulently anti-Catholic Scottish Presbyterian Whiggamores—wanted war with France and wanted James excluded from the succession. Charles's numerous supporters, increasingly called Tories after Irish Roman Catholics, claimed that the French threat was overstated and insisted on James's indefeasible hereditary right to the throne. Because of the high level of ideological tension, and the unprecedented strength of political opposition, Charles II was forced to call three parliamentary elections in three years, which succeeded in energizing the political nation. Huge numbers of people petitioned and addressed in support of both parties. Eventually, Charles II and his Tory supporters were able to defeat the Whigs both in the arenas of high politics and in the court of public opinion. Many came to believe that the Whigs sought to reinitiate England's civil wars. Whig leaders, including the Earl of Shaftesbury and his secretary, John Locke, fled to the Netherlands.

In 1683, a failed plot by radical Whigs to assassinate Charles II and his brother decisively turned much of the public against the Whigs. Charles was freed to initiate a widespread campaign against the parliamentary constituencies, or corporations, that had returned Whig members to the Parliaments of 1679 to 1681. Prosecutions against religious Dissenters, thought to be the natural allies of the Whigs, were significantly ramped up. The king was able to restore strict control of the press. Roger L'Estrange served both as licenser of the press and as chief government propagandist through his widely distributed newspaper, the *Observator in Dialogue* (see Document 37).

Charles II died in February 1685 and was peacefully succeeded by his brother, James II. At this moment, the English monarchy was poised to achieve the same kind of absolute political authority enjoyed in France, Denmark, and Sweden. A poorly planned and badly mismanaged rebellion in June 1685 led by Charles II's illegitimate son, James Duke of Monmouth, only strengthened James II's position. The Duke of Monmouth landed in the west of England in mid-June with a handful of men. While he quickly gathered support from the religiously persecuted Protestant Nonconformists (those who were unable to conform to the rituals or accept the hierarchy of the Church of England), he never achieved support from the politically powerful western gentry and nobility. This was in part because the Duke of Monmouth portrayed his rebellion solely as a war of religion. He insisted that he was the proper heir to the throne and that James II's title was a Roman Catholic hoax. For the Duke of Monmouth, his was a struggle about whether England would have a Protestant or a Catholic monarchy. Unfortunately for Monmouth, many in England — especially many of the middle and higher echelons of society — believed the lesson of the previous century of European history was that wars of religion resulted only in massive bloodshed and political confusion.

James II's army fairly quickly defeated the Duke of Monmouth's ragtag forces. As soon as James captured his nephew, he had him beheaded and had his lord chancellor prosecute Monmouth's supporters to the fullest extent of the law. James used the event to point out the inadequacies of England's county militias. England could only be safe at home and abroad, he argued, with a modern standing army. He needed an army, James II argued, modeled on that constructed by the powerful Louis XIV of France.

Over the next three years, James II succeeded in creating a modern state apparatus with extensive powers. Not only did he claim extensive political powers, but he used these powers. Towns throughout England, from Berwick to Portsmouth, from Plymouth to York, from Chester to Hull, hosted large military garrisons. James worked closely with longtime acquaintance Samuel Pepys to build up and equip an efficient navy. James used the post office to circulate government propaganda and to survey the writings of any politician whose loyalty he suspected. In theory, James created the Ecclesiastical Commission to run the Protestant Church of England since he, as a practicing Roman Catholic, could not. In practice, the Ecclesiastical Commission cracked down on political commentary emanating from England's pulpits. Since it interpreted criticism of the Catholic Church as political criticism of the king's faith, Protestant clerics were severely limited in their freedom to preach.

James II also promoted an innovative religious policy. The new king was determined to restore the Roman Catholic Church to its rightful place in English religious life. He knew, however, that the overwhelming majority of English men and women were devout Protestants with profound anti-Catholic prejudices who would not accept Catholicism as the official state religion. Therefore he simply hoped to free Catholicism from legal and political prohibition in England. When it became clear that no amount of personal lobbying would convince his Tory supporters to vote in Parliament for a repeal of the laws condemning Catholics and Protestant Nonconformists, James turned his hopes to his former enemies: Protestant Nonconformists. James issued two Declarations of Indulgence (see one in Document 32) annulling the penalties against Catholics and Protestant Dissenters (Nonconformists). At the same time, he initiated a widespread campaign to secure a Parliament that would reverse the older parliamentary statutes. Whereas contemporary politicians conduct political surveys to fine-tune their political message, James II conducted a massive political survey to fine-tune the electorate. He asked politicians and potential politicians whether they would support repeal of the penal laws against Protestant Dissenting and Roman Catholic religious worship and repeal of the Test Acts (enacted in 1673) against Protestant Dissenting and Roman Catholic political participation. Those who refused to support his policies were removed from positions of political and social authority.

James II's newly intrusive and powerful state represented an affront to the ideas and way of life of many in England. For others, James's active attempts to modernize the English polity in the fashion of Louis XIV's France represented a real opportunity. Some old Tories were caught in between: They found James II's actions abhorrent but could not justify resisting an anointed king. But almost no one in England could refrain from taking sides. James II succeeded in polarizing his nation.

The rapid collapse of James II's position in England in the winter of 1688–89 has masked for many historians the seriousness of James II's program. James almost succeeded in creating a modernized English state with a coherent foreign and imperial policy (see "Revolution in Politics" below). James did have significant support for his policies both within England and in Scotland and Ireland. That Jacobites (supporters of James II's claim) fought in Ireland and Scotland to restore their king was a strategic decision, not a recognition of their numerical weakness in England. James II had many supporters within England. Not only did he have Catholic friends in England, but among his supporters were Quakers, such as William Penn, and members of the Church of England, such as the Duke of Beaufort, the Earl of Huntingdon, and the Earl of Clarendon. Many old Tories who were critical of James II's modernizing policies came to support their former king once it became clear that William III and his supporters aimed not only to reverse James's policies but also to adopt a modernizing program of their own. These Jacobites were well aware that the Revolution of 1688–89 was much more than a constitutional struggle.

REVOLUTION IN POLITICS

Ignoring the rapidly changing nature of English society, the traditional story of the Revolution of 1688–89 has begun and ended with the constitution. The Declaration of Rights of February 1689 (Document 12), which became the Bill of Rights when it was given the status of a parliamentary statute in December 1689, is normally seen to have encapsulated the essence of the revolution. The revolution did systematically codify the political rights of Englishmen. In fact, the English Bill of Rights was a major influence among the American colonists in drafting their Declaration of Independence in 1776.

Yet Edmund Burke and many historians who have followed him have suggested that the Bill of Rights only restated old law. He was right, of course, to point out that many things insisted on in the Bill of Rights had precedents in English history. The Petition of Right of 1628, for example, had already established some of these important rights. Nevertheless, there were some distinctly novel elements in the Declaration of Rights, elements that reflected specific discontent with the rule of James II. The Declaration of Rights emphasized changes in the nature of the succession to the English crown by excluding James II's son; it insisted that kings did not have the right to dispense with or suspend laws passed by Parliament; and it prohibited the monarch from raising a permanent standing army. At the same time, the Declaration and Bill of Rights insisted more forcefully than ever that elections to Parliament must be free of governmental interference.

Not only did the Declaration and Bill of Rights insist that a wide variety of rights were held by all Englishmen, but defenders of the new regime described the nature of government in terms very different from those used by propagandists for James II. After one of the more serious rebellions against Charles II's regime in 1683—now known as the Rye House Plot—Oxford University banned a series of political and religious propositions. In essence, one of England's two universities, which was itself very closely tied to the government, insisted that England was governed by a divine-right monarch who was answerable to no one but God. All political resistance and most forms of political criticism were illegal. That monarch, the decrees implied, was supported by the Protestant Church of England. All religious meetings outside of that church were simultaneously illegal and a potential subversive threat to the regime. After James II's accession and the short-lived and ill-fated rebellion led by his nephew, James Duke of Monmouth, in the summer of 1685, these same themes were enunciated in sermon after sermon across the country. After the Revolution of 1688–89, by contrast, a variety of different justifications for the legitimacy of the regime were heard. For example, some argued that James II had broken the original contract with the people and hence had been deposed. Others maintained that James II had providentially deserted his country, rendering the throne vacant. While the notion that the power of England's kings was limited by law by no means monopolized the ideological landscape, it did have a prominence in official circles that was unknown during the reigns of Charles II and James II.

In a narrowly constitutional and political sense, the Revolution of

1688–89 did alter the ideological orientation of England's polity. The Declaration of Rights did advance new rights and clarify old ones. That many moderate supporters of the revolution objected to some of the language in the declaration makes clear that this document was not merely restating old law. However, it is surely correct to suggest, as Colley Cibber did, that the English had frequently made claims to their rights in the past. None of the arguments for limited monarchy published in pamphlets or preached in sermons were all that novel. The same arguments had been advanced during the parliamentary struggles of the 1620s, during the English Civil War in the 1640s, and during the debates over the succession during Charles II's reign. What was new, as Cibber noted, was that these rights were given substance (see Document 5). Legal guarantees meant little if the king was able to ignore the law. A theory of limited monarchy did not constrain the king if he was not obliged in practice as well as in theory to convene Parliament.[6]

Why, in fact, did English monarchs follow the law after the revolution? What gave the Declaration of Rights substance? Three revolutionary changes in the orientation of the English state had the combined effect of compelling English kings to be limited monarchs: the radical reorientation of English foreign policy, English political economy, and the Church of England. These revolutionary changes are what distinguish the Revolution of 1688–89 as the first modern revolution.

REVOLUTION IN FOREIGN POLICY

The English in the late seventeenth century were not an intellectually insular people. They had a sophisticated understanding of European and extra-European affairs. Throughout the late seventeenth century, newspapers were filled with stories detailing political and military developments on the European continent. Coffeehouses were abuzz with gossip about Louis XIV's most recent escapade, the latest Spanish court intrigue, and the most recent Ottoman military exploit. English country gentlemen routinely subscribed to European as well as English newspapers. Sermons were liberally sprinkled with references to

---

[6]Both Charles II and James II were required by the Triennial Act of 1664 to convene Parliament every three years. There was nothing, however, that could *compel* them to do so.

religious and secular European trends. Bookshops in the capital and provincial centers stocked a wide variety of works from European presses.

When the English turned their thoughts to continental affairs, they were usually struck by the great struggle taking place between Europe's economic dynamo, the Dutch Republic, and Europe's greatest military power, the France of Louis XIV. To James II, like his older brother, Charles II, the Dutch Republic offered a very troubling prospect. After Charles II was restored to the throne in 1660, the Netherlands immediately provided an offshore home to his political and ideological enemies. It was for this reason that Charles II, with James at his side, fought two unsuccessful wars against the Dutch Republic (1665–67, 1672–74). When James II succeeded his brother in 1685, the Netherlands hosted a wide array of his opponents. Gilbert Burnet, a leading opponent of James II's religious policies, had fled there, as had John Locke, one of James II's greatest political critics. The passenger barges, town squares, and coffeehouses of the greatest Dutch towns hosted a wide range of English and Scottish political exiles.

English exiles fled to the Dutch Republic because it represented the political antithesis of the later Stuart monarchy. Whereas Charles II and James II claimed to rule England by hereditary divine right, the Netherlands was manifestly a republic. It was true that James II's son-in-law, William III of Orange, played an extremely important role in the politics of the Netherlands. Yet his role was not that of a king. He came to political authority on a wave of popular sentiment in 1672. His control over the Dutch military was always subject to the oversight of the Dutch States General.[7] Real political power lay in the individual assembly of each of the seven Dutch provinces. Holland, the richest and demographically the largest of the Dutch provinces, had a disproportionate influence on Dutch policy. And Holland was extremely wary of allowing any member of the House of Orange to appear anything like a king. From the perspective of James II in London, the Dutch Republic provided a dangerous political example for his countrymen and for Europe as a whole. The Dutch Republic appeared to James and his supporters as a political cancer.

The religious policy of the Dutch polity also provided a clear con-

---

[7]The Dutch States General was equivalent to a parliament that met in The Hague. Unlike the English Parliament, however, members were not directly elected. The States General was, in effect, a meeting of the representatives of the seven Dutch provinces.

trast with the coercive state church in England. The Dutch Republic (or the United Provinces of the Netherlands) was the most religiously tolerant country in Europe. Many of Europe's religious refugees fled to the Netherlands. Mennonites went to the Dutch Republic when they were evicted from Germany. Jews fled to the Netherlands from Spain and Portugal. Thousands of French Protestants, called Huguenots, came to the Netherlands as they were increasingly persecuted in Louis XIV's France. And the Netherlands provided a refuge for English Protestants who could not stomach the rituals and requirements of the Church of England. Quakers, Baptists, Presbyterians, and Congregationalists all made their homes in Amsterdam, Rotterdam, and Utrecht.

While it may be hard for us to imagine, the Dutch Republic in the late seventeenth century was also a great military and naval power. The Dutch had achieved their independence in the early seventeenth century by defeating the most powerful European monarchy of that era, Spain. The Dutch military had set the European standard for precise drilling and training. Its methods were adopted and mimicked all over Europe. But the real Dutch strength was at sea. Dutch naval prowess was proverbial in the seventeenth century. Dutch traders were prominent in the West Indies, on the west coast of Africa, in European waters, and above all in the East Indies. The Dutch East India Company had established a colonial capital at Batavia (modern Jakarta) in Indonesia and had come to dominate the European trade along the southern coast of India, Persia, and Japan. The extent of their maritime empire made plausible Stuart fears that the Dutch would soon achieve universal dominion based on commercial hegemony.

From James II's perspective, the Dutch polity needed to be destroyed. England could never be stable as long as the Dutch Republic sheltered his enemies, financed their plots, and promoted such dangerous political ideas. Dutch commercial hegemony convinced James and his advisers that failure to act may well mean slow but certain economic strangulation for England. Court sentiment grew that James II must finish the job that Charles II had begun in his two inconclusive wars against the Dutch. Court memoranda circulated arguing that the Netherlands must be destroyed. In preparation for this final blow at the heart of the ideologically threatening Dutch Republic, James carefully built up his navy. Meanwhile, his propagandists spewed forth poems and pamphlets castigating the Dutch for their political and religious corruption. In January 1688, James recalled the three English regiments that had traditionally protected the Dutch Republic against threats from continental powers. By the spring, most political gossips were certain war would come that summer or autumn (see Documents 15–20). And come it did, in the form of a Dutch preemptive first strike in November 1688.

While Charles II and James II were convinced that the Netherlands posed the greatest threat to England, most of their subjects increasingly believed that France was the greater threat to the English way of life. Louis XIV was the most powerful king in Europe.[8] His soldiers numbered in the hundreds of thousands. James II's army, by contrast, was only about forty thousand strong. French diplomats had succeeded in bullying and cajoling much of Europe into acquiescing to the inevitability of French power. Already by the 1670s, most European observers were convinced that France had replaced Spain as the greatest monarchy in Europe. Many believed that it was only a matter of time before Louis XIV would proclaim himself "universal monarch."

For many in England, the regime of Louis XIV was a greater ideological danger than the Dutch Republic. Louis XIV appeared to recognize no limits on his power. There was no parliament to check his ambitions. There was no law that could bind him. When Louis XIV revoked the Edict of Nantes in 1685—an edict issued by Louis's grandfather Henri IV in 1598 that guaranteed certain rights to the French Protestant community—it seemed to many that he had overturned France's equivalent of the Magna Carta. Louis XIV was the embodiment of a king who recognized no earthly superior (see Documents 21–22).

From the 1670s, the English were increasingly concerned about Louis XIV's economic practices as well. Louis and his great minister, Jean-Baptiste Colbert, had created a number of successful national manufactures. They had also promoted a remarkably thoroughgoing series of tariff and nontariff trade barriers. The result was that English manufacturers were unable to sell their goods in the lucrative French marketplace. Many cloth-making regions in England that had depended on French outlets for their products had to reorient their trade. By contrast, England was a great consumer of French luxury goods, such as silks and red wines. Many commentators remarked on the ubiquity of French fashions in London and English provincial cities.

Louis XIV's religious policies were just as terrifying to many in England. Not only was Louis XIV a committed Catholic, but he was

---

[8]See William Beik, *Louis XIV and Absolutism* (Boston: Bedford/St. Martin's, 2000).

committed to the notion that only religious uniformity was compatible with a strong state. French Calvinists, who had long enjoyed specific religious guarantees, were offered the choice of conversion or annihilation. Thousands fled. Thousands more converted. For some in England, Louis XIV's actions proved that no Roman Catholic monarch could be trusted. For most, however, the revocation of the Edict of Nantes and the subsequent forcible conversions demonstrated that it was impossible to maintain religious liberty without first guaranteeing civil liberty. Religious toleration would always be fragile under absolutist regimes.

For the English, the choice between a French or a Dutch alignment was much more than a question of geopolitics. It was the choice between two very different ways of life. It was a choice with stark contrasts not unlike that offered to many Europeans at the height of the cold war. With each accretion of French power in the late seventeenth century, more and more English citizens concluded that France—much more than the Netherlands—posed a threat to the English polity and society. In fact, many hoped that when James II, a man with a sterling reputation as a military leader, came to the throne, England would at long last go to war with France. However, James, unlike most of his countrymen, felt that the Dutch Republic was a far greater threat. His perceived appeasement of France played no small role in turning the English against his regime. It was therefore one of the primary aims of the revolutionaries of 1688–89 to reverse England's foreign policy. The first prong of the revolutionary program of 1688–89 was to declare war against France (see Documents 23–24). In fact, William's prime qualification for the job of English king in the eyes of many was his lifelong commitment to containing the growing power of Louis XIV. By bringing William to the throne in 1689, the revolutionaries had achieved their first objective: they had radically reoriented English foreign policy.

REVOLUTION IN POLITICAL ECONOMY

The Revolution of 1688–89 dramatically reoriented England's social and economic policy. Both James II and William III had sophisticated and activist economic programs. Like modern leaders, and unlike medieval ones, they sought to improve their subjects' material well-being. While the two kings disagreed profoundly in their ideological assumptions and their preferred policies, they agreed that a successful political economic program was a vital element of statecraft. Historians, however, have ignored this central element of the revolution because they assume that the late-seventeenth-century state functioned like a medieval state. They assume that debates about political economy did not begin until the late eighteenth century.

Just as England's economy changed rapidly in the seventeenth century, so did the nature of English statecraft. Wars in the late seventeenth century were very different from military struggles of the late Middle Ages or the Renaissance. Armies were much larger. The fighting season was much longer. Set-piece battles had, by and large, been replaced by long sieges. Late-seventeenth-century wars were wars of attrition. Increasingly, this meant that the most powerful state was that state that could marshal the greatest financial resources. Money, in the language of the seventeenth century, provided the sinews of power (see Document 10).

Charles II and James II were well aware that changes in the nature of warfare, coupled with the widening of economic horizons, meant that the nature of politics in the late seventeenth century was very different from what it had been in their father's day. Charles II was fascinated by new manufacturing techniques. He eagerly visited the launching of new ships. His brother, James, was more involved still in the machinery of the modern state. James served as director of England's Royal African Company in the 1670s and 1680s. He invested heavily in East India Company stock. He befriended leading members of England's increasingly powerful merchant community. James also did all he could to modernize England's navy with the help of a trusted civil servant, the famous diarist Samuel Pepys. James knew that to be a successful modern monarch, above all to be one who could compete with the Dutch, he needed to have a modern economy and a modern navy.

Making economic policy in the late seventeenth century, much like developing an economic agenda today, required selecting from among a variety of plausible policies. Again, much like in the contemporary world, a politician's ideological predisposition informed his or her economic agenda. James II's political economic agenda was simultaneously informed by his experience with the East India and Royal African companies and his commitment to the notion that the Dutch Republic was England's great political rival. By the 1680s, James had developed a coherent, sophisticated, and thoroughly modern economic and imperial strategy.

James and his advisers, such as the East India merchant Josiah

Child, the Africa merchant Benjamin Bathurst, and the Lord Chancellor George Jefferies, believed that the basis of all property and wealth was land. It was land that provided the agrarian base for all economies. Coveted luxuries like tobacco, sugar, and spices were all products of the land. Since the amount of land in the world was necessarily finite, the struggle for prosperity was a zero-sum game—what one nation gained, another lost (see Documents 25–26). James therefore sought to rationalize and promote England's imperial possessions. In North America, James, while still Duke of York, amalgamated New York, Rhode Island, Connecticut, and Massachusetts to create the Dominion of New England in 1684. He sought to create a parallel Dominion of the West Indies. And he began to create a new Dominion of India based in Bombay. Because James assumed the viciousness of international competition, the English monarch worked with the African and East India companies, as well as his Board of Trade, to ensure that these colonies would be militarily self-sufficient. James felt deeply that economic and imperial policy was a central part of the royal prerogative. Trading companies and their territories, therefore, answered to the king alone, and not to Parliament. In the colonies, there was only the king's law; Parliament had no jurisdiction outside of England.

James and his advisers were convinced that his great imperial competitors were the Dutch. This was, in part, because James felt that the key to imperial success lay in India, not in the West Indies. It was Indian cloth and spices that yielded the largest profits for the merchants and that guaranteed the largest customs revenues for the crown. In the East Indies, there was little question that the Dutch were England's greatest European rivals. This was less true in the West Indies after the demise of the Dutch colony in Brazil and the conquest of New Amsterdam (New York) by the English. In Europe, too, Dutch manufacturers competed with the English for increasingly dwindling markets.

James II's economic policy had clear domestic corollaries as well. Since land, and not manufacturing, was the basis of wealth, James sought to promote England's landed gentlemen at the expense of the newly developing manufacturing sectors. Land was lightly taxed, whereas the hearth tax imposed after Charles II's restoration heavily assessed those who needed heat to manufacture their products. Sheffield ironworkers, for example, deeply resented the tax policies of the later Stuart monarchs. James also sought to promote England's fishing industry, a sort of farming of the sea. Here, too, English fishermen were in desperate competition with the Dutch for the European herring trade. Indeed, some of James II's economic advisers argued that Dutch wealth depended on the riches generated by the fisheries that the Dutch had stolen from the English.

James II and his friends from the committee rooms of the Africa and East India companies did not, however, hold a monopoly on economic ideas in the late seventeenth century. Their ideas were opposed by another powerful, wealthy, and influential group of merchants. Many of these merchants had been purged from the East India Company in the 1670s and 1680s, and many had ties to England's manufacturing community or were themselves manufacturers. Unlike the circle around James II, they argued that the basis of property and wealth was human labor rather than land. Since wealth was created by work, it was not necessarily finite; it was infinitely expandable. As a result, economic competition was not a zero-sum game; it was possible for several nations to become wealthier simultaneously. Within each kingdom, manufacturing would drive the national economy. As workers produced more, they would have more disposable income with which to purchase more goods, in turn stimulating more industries. In this view, there were no limits to economic growth.

From these assumptions grew an alternative understanding of economic and imperial policy. Proponents of this view argued that the key to England's long-term prosperity was in manufacturing. Therefore the East India trade, a trade that imported finished calicoes and other cheap cloths that competed with the English clothing industry, should be discouraged. The West Indies, which produced sugar to be refined in England and tobacco that could be reexported throughout Europe, was another matter. Similarly, proponents of this view understood the international economic order very differently. Since, in their view, trade was infinitely expandable, these merchants did not see Dutch economic prosperity as threatening. The French, by contrast, were a danger. French protectionist policies excluded English manufactures from French markets. And the diplomatic pressure the French were able to exert on other countries closed even more markets to the English. Unsurprisingly, many of the loudest proponents of this view were merchants who once traded heavily with France (see Documents 27 and 29).

On the domestic front, proponents of this view shared with their opponents the conviction that the state should intervene in the economy. But unlike James II and his supporters, those who thought that wealth was infinitely expandable argued that government economic policy should favor the manufacturing sector rather than the landed elite. They hated the hearth tax for harming manufacturers and longed for a return to the high land taxes of the 1640s and 1650s. Supporters of the manufacturing sector became increasingly frustrated with James II's economic policies. They detested the favoritism shown to the East India and Royal African companies. They lamented James's acquiescence to Louis XIV's protectionist measures. They resented the steady drumbeat for war against the Dutch. Unsurprisingly, many of James's economic opponents began to turn decisively against the regime, sending money to William of Orange in 1688, thinking that only he could remedy their plight.

After William and Mary succeeded in overthrowing James II, the defenders of England's manufacturing sector gained the upper hand. The same Parliament that placed William on the throne reversed James II's taxation policies. In April 1689, the hearth tax was repealed, and in December 1689, a land tax was instituted for the first time since the 1650s. Many then turned their attention to the monopoly held by the East India Company. In session after session of Parliament in the 1690s, proposals were put forward to disband or reorganize the East India Company. While the company's opponents succeeded in establishing the principle that all companies were subject to Parliament and English law, the company itself remained. It survived in large part because in a time of warfare against the French, the East India Company had the potential to offer the government large loans to pay for an increasingly expensive war. The company's opponents, however, merely shifted their ground. They succeeded in limiting the East India Company's influence by establishing the Bank of England in 1694, which simultaneously loaned the government money to pay for the war[9] and helped redistribute money in the form of loans to the manufacturing sector. The bank—supported politically by James II's opponents, such as John Locke and Isaac Newton, and financially by the old enemies of the East India Company—was based on the notion that England's economic future lay in the manufacturing sector and not exclusively in the land (see Document 28).

The Revolution of 1688–89 completely reoriented England's political economy. James II had pursued an imperial policy emphasizing the importance of land and the East Indies. The new regime pointed England toward manufacturing and the West Indies. James II's regime had adopted economic views not unlike those of Colbert in France and

---

[9]The bank, however, was answerable to Parliament, not to the king alone. The king could not simply seize money.

believed that the Dutch were its greatest economic rivals. William and Mary, unsurprisingly, drew their economic inspiration from the Netherlands and argued that French protectionism posed the greatest threat to England's economic future.

REVOLUTION IN THE CHURCH

While warfare and political economy had changed substantially over the course of the seventeenth century, the Church retained a socially and culturally central role in the lives of the English. All English men and women were compelled by law to attend Church of England services every Sunday. All other forms of religious worship were illegal. The Revolution of 1688–89 radically shifted power within the Church of England and eliminated many of the prohibitions against worship outside that Church.

After the Restoration in 1660, Charles II promoted a very specific kind of churchman to the highest ranks in the Church of England. These men came to be known as *high churchmen*. Those who were preferred to episcopal sees and rich deaneries were by and large men who condemned the temporary disestablishment of the Church of England in the 1640s and 1650s. They blamed the interregnum for unleashing a series of unwholesome and dangerous religious sects. Presbyterians, Independents, Baptists, Quakers, Ranters, and Fifth Monarchy Men all preached and published in the 1640s and 1650s. While the Act of Uniformity of 1662 had outlawed these and other sects and had firmly reestablished the Church of England, the Anglican clergy knew full well that religious dissent had not been eviscerated. These men believed that religious dissent was both politically subversive and spiritually dangerous. Religious Dissenters, they argued, actively disobeyed the king's law and had been responsible for initiating the civil war that ended with the execution of Charles I. Dissenters, the high churchmen claimed, refused to obey human laws that contradicted their interpretation of divine law. Since there could be only one true church, many high church divines contended, religious Dissenters were necessarily guilty of the sin of schism. These high church divines therefore adamantly opposed any loosening of church requirements. They rejected calls for comprehension—making the definition of Church of England practice looser so as to include moderate Presbyterians—because they believed strongly in the efficacy of their version of church ritual. They opposed toleration—legalizing religious worship outside the Church of England—because there could be only one true path to salvation (see Document 30). High churchmen were deeply devoted to improving the ties between the priest and his parochial community. But for them, pastoral care meant ensuring that parishioners were orthodox and frequent communicants as a prerequisite to receiving poor relief.

The high churchmen did hold the majority of desirable church benefices during the reigns of Charles II and James II. From the 1670s, they were able to work very closely with powerful laymen to secure the most desirable posts. Archbishop of Canterbury Gilbert Sheldon and his successor, William Sancroft, did much to improve the quality of the Church of England clergy through their pastoral letters and episcopal visitations. They also worked extremely hard to maintain its ideological purity.

The high churchmen did not, however, monopolize all positions within the Church of England. A number of clerics with a distinctly different vision for the Church retained both posts and influence. These men came to be known as *low churchmen*. This group of men had, by and large, not gone into exile in the 1640s and 1650s. Many of them had in fact been educated at Oxford or Cambridge during the interregnum, when the Church of England had lost its monopoly over the universities. While they themselves conformed to the Church of England, many of these low churchmen came from families that were more associated with the parliamentary and puritan sides in the English civil wars. And, perhaps tellingly, many of these men served as parish priests in London.

This group of men, which included Gilbert Burnet, Simon Patrick, and the postrevolutionary Archbishop of Canterbury John Tillotson, held very different views from their opponents. They argued that while there was only one true church, that true church would not be marked by persecution. They also came to believe that a religious man or woman was characterized less by the purity of his or her doctrine than by his or her moral character. Given these premises, they did not believe that religious dissent was an act of political obstinacy, but rather a conscientious following of deeply felt convictions (see Document 31).

Low churchmen differed radically from their high church brethren on three important issues. First, they argued in favor of a broader, comprehensive Church of England that included moderate Dissenters and toleration for those who could not be so accommodated. Since dissent was an act of conscience, and conscience could not be coerced, the low churchmen insisted that the Church needed to make space for as many conscientious believers as it could. There would always be those who would remain unable to worship in the Church of England, but it was better by far to allow them to live comfortable and productive lives in England than to compel them to be exiles. Second, they maintained that clergy had no role to play in politics. They insisted that the Bible had not specified any particular form of government as being best. Governments, they maintained, played no part in the salvation of subjects. The low churchmen thus asserted that rebellion was never justified by the claim that the king was a heretic. They also insisted, however, that rulers were responsible for promotion of the common good. Low churchmen denied that any prince was answerable only to God. A tyrant could and should be resisted for secular reasons. Third, the low churchmen had a different view of pastoral care. They agreed with the high churchmen that the great weakness of earlier Protestants was their neglect of the social and moral well-being of their parishioners. However, unlike the high churchmen, they argued that moral and physical amelioration had to precede doctrinal catechism. A starving man, they reasoned, would accede to whatever doctrines would gain him food. Using poor relief as an incentive to attend church did not create sincere believers.

The reign of James II was a trying period for both high and low churchmen. James's Declarations of Indulgence of 1687 (see Document 32) and 1688 and his patronage of Catholic missionaries created a temporary alliance of these two groups. They both feared that James would attempt to recatholicize England. However, their temporary alliance should not blind us to their real religious differences.

From 1689, the fortunes of the high and low churchmen were reversed. Many high churchmen could not take the oaths of allegiance to the new regime because doing so would imply that resistance to a legitimate monarch could be justified. Many more grudgingly took the new oaths, arguing that William and Mary had in fact been crowned king and queen. Whether or not the new regime was legitimate was not a proper question, they said. They took the oaths in the belief that some government was preferable to anarchy. There were eighteen episcopal vacancies for the new monarchs to fill between 1689 and 1692. William and Mary had an opportunity to reshape the Church of England in their own image. They did not let the opportunity slip. They overwhelmingly appointed low churchmen to the vacant episcopal sees. While the low churchmen failed to get a comprehension bill through Parliament, they did secure the passage of the Toleration Act in 1689, which guaranteed freedom of religious worship for all non-Roman Catholic Christians. They also were among the many in Parliament who in 1696 passed a parliamentary act declaring that William was the lawful and rightful king of England, not merely the king whom the English happened to have. They gained parliamentary legitimacy for the political resistance that had spawned the revolution.[10] And the new low church bishops played a prominent role in promoting the reformation-of-manners movement, a campaign to improve the moral quality of English life. Both lay and clerical low churchmen had worked closely with Protestant Nonconformists to overthrow James II. After his departure they were able to fundamentally transform the Church of England.

INTERPRETING THE REVOLUTION OF 1688–1689

Why did the Revolution of 1688–89 make the rights of Englishmen tangible? Why did the events of that time finally make real the rights so many Englishmen had long claimed to be theirs in theory? The answer lies beyond the sphere of narrow constitutional history. For financial and commercial reasons, William and Mary and their successors were compelled to accept the Bill of Rights as a limitation on their power. The massive cost of the wars against France compelled them to rely on Parliament as an institution for financial support. English monarchs had to convene Parliament on a regular basis to authorize levying taxes to support the cost of war against the world's greatest power. By committing themselves to the promotion of a commercial society that privileged manufacturing, the English monarchs also committed themselves to protecting the rights enumerated in the Bill of Rights. What merchant or tradesman would invest in any business enterprise without guarantees that their property would be secure?

By promoting low churchmen, William and Mary also committed themselves to a religious party that insisted that government existed to serve the people and was ultimately answerable to the people. The

---

[10]Low churchmen argued that only by severing the close ties between the Church of England and the state could the Church be freed to pursue its proper pursuits of salvation and moral improvement. While they argued that political resistance was legitimate, they advanced that argument not as churchmen, but as Englishmen. They referred not to divine law, but to natural law and parliamentary statutes. They argued that high churchmen erred in positing that the Bible gave positive arguments for any one form of government. The Bible, in the view of the low churchmen, offered no prescription for politics.

revolution that had taken place in the Church of England ensured that preachers throughout England would frequently remind their parishioners that they had a right to resist a government that broke the law.

From as early as 1689, however, many interpreters of the Revolution of 1688–89 have insisted that there was nothing modern or innovative about it. Some have claimed that James II was overthrown by the opponents of his advocacy of religious toleration. Upon his invasion of Ireland in 1689 in an attempt to retake his kingdoms, James II argued that he had been overthrown by a reactionary religious faction. He claimed that he was stripped of his crown by high churchmen who resented his policy of religious toleration by royal edict. James had, in fact, issued two Declarations of Indulgence in England (1687 and 1688) that had in effect nullified the 1662 Act of Uniformity. All English people were thereby allowed to worship at the churches of their choice. Initially, it is true, the declarations were greeted with euphoria by the long-persecuted religious dissenters. Soon, however, they came to realize that their religious freedom depended on James II's claim that he could dispense with parliamentary statutes. Increasingly, religious dissenters realized that if the king had the right to nullify one parliamentary statute, by the same logic he could render invalid all laws. By June 1688, many religious Dissenters joined members of the Church of England in denouncing the arrest and trial of seven Anglican bishops for refusing to read the second Declaration of Indulgence. They understood that the bishops' refusal was in fact a defense of civil rights, rather than a condemnation of religious toleration. Dissenters had become convinced that there could be no religious liberty without civil liberty (see Documents 33–34).

Other scholars have suggested that the Revolution of 1688–89 was no more than an anti-Catholic coup d'état. The Protestant English, these scholars argue, were pathologically anti-Catholic. The events of 1688–89 merely replaced a Roman Catholic monarch with an acceptable Protestant one. The revolution, in this view, was a late phase of the European wars of religion. Elegant and simple as this explanation is, it fails to take account of Catholic attitudes or to explain the nature of the postrevolutionary regime. Roman Catholics were deeply divided over James II's policies. Many old English Catholic families, while delighted to have freedom of religious worship, were themselves worried about James II's absolutism. They soon found a leader in the papal nuncio who was invited to England by James. The nuncio, infuriated by the pro-French policies being pursued by James and his pro-French advisers, led a group of Catholic gentry and noblemen in opposition to royal policies. Religious bigotry lay behind only a fraction of the opposition to James II (see Document 35). More significantly, the new regime did not pursue anti-Catholic policies. The war against France was fought in alliance with the Catholic Holy Roman emperor and the Catholic king of Spain. William intervened to prevent illegal actions against Roman Catholic civilians (see Document 36). While the Act of Toleration did exclude them, many Roman Catholics claimed that in practice they enjoyed more religious freedom than at any time since the reign of Henry VIII (1509–1547).

Late-seventeenth-century England was not a secular society. People went to church regularly and believed deeply in God. But the Revolution of 1688–89 was not a war of religion. William and Mary were uninterested in pursuing religious crusades at home or abroad. The revolution was perhaps the first political struggle of the Enlightenment,[11] a struggle in which the political rights and material welfare of the people were at stake; it was certainly not the last battle of the age of religious wars.

THE FIRST MODERN REVOLUTION

The Revolution of 1688–89 was the first modern revolution. It was not, however, a revolution that pitted a modernizing faction against a reactionary one. Both sides advocated modernization. Both James II and William III accepted that political economy was a central element of modern statecraft. Whereas Renaissance politicians had felt that their responsibilities were to promote the religious and political virtue of their subjects, James and William both believed that they were also responsible for promoting their economic welfare. Modern statecraft, they both felt, included political economy.

James and William simply had very different visions for a modernized England. James, deeply impressed by the success and grandeur of Louis XIV, opted for a large, powerful bureaucratic state that relied on land for its political power. He envisaged an English future that included an expanding empire. James felt that political power depended on a strong state that was religiously pluralist, but politically uniform. A modern sovereign, he believed, needed absolute and unquestioned

---

[11]The Enlightenment was a broad-based and multinational eighteenth-century movement aiming at improving the human condition in this world. Many of the central concerns of the Enlightenment—political economy, the relationship between church and state, and the power of the king—were central concerns of the Revolution of 1688–89.

authority to make and enforce policy. This sovereign, James argued, needed a large bureaucracy and a powerful permanent army to enforce his authority at home and abroad. Those modern institutions could, in turn, best be maintained by the income generated from imperial trade, principally with the East Indies.

William, by contrast, drew inspiration for his version of the modern state from his native Dutch Republic. He agreed with James that a powerful state required a large bureaucracy and a permanent military force. William committed himself, however, to a political economy that emphasized manufacturing as the primary source of national wealth. As a result, William was committed to recognizing legal protections for property and to creating institutions like the Bank of England that promoted manufacturing. Unlike Charles II and James II, William was committed to toleration by statute. He and his supporters maintained that only parliamentary guarantees for religious freedom would attract the labor pool necessary for work in England's industries.

These two contrasting political visions are encapsulated in the writings of two of the most effective pamphleteers of the late seventeenth century: Roger L'Estrange and John Locke. Locke has been widely viewed as one of the first great thinkers of the modern age. L'Estrange, now almost forgotten, offered an alternative vision of modernity. In a series of newspapers, newsletters, and pamphlets, L'Estrange, who had served Charles II as licenser of the press,[12] defended the ideological vision of James II and his elder brother. L'Estrange emphasized that no government could be stable that tolerated political dissent. This was in large part why he castigated England's religious Nonconformists, who objected publicly to the laws prohibiting religious worship outside the Church of England. This was also why L'Estrange so detested the Dutch. In political economy, L'Estrange emphasized the importance of seizing as many of the world's limited resources as possible. L'Estrange's adamant defense of a royal fishery was based on the assumption that wealth was finite. By reclaiming their coastal fish farm, the English were necessarily reclaiming that scarce resource from their Dutch rivals (see Documents 37–38).

John Locke, by contrast, published a set of deeply influential pamphlets in the immediate aftermath of the Revolution of 1688–89. He argued that because governments were created to serve the needs of the people, the people therefore served as a necessary and legitimate

---

[12] L'Estrange was responsible for reading and approving, as politically and religiously orthodox, all books printed in England.

check on the authority of the sovereign. In fact, he argued that government was initially created to protect the property that came into existence through human labor. Locke, who was one of the earliest supporters of the Bank of England, helped promote English manufactures during his term on England's Board of Trade. He had developed a deep distaste for the French regime during his travels there in the 1670s and was an ardent supporter of war against France. Only by limiting the power of Louis XIV, he argued, could the liberties of England and all Europe be guaranteed. John Locke, who returned to England from his exile in the Dutch Republic just after James II's flight to France, became for many the ideological voice of the postrevolutionary regime.

Scholars usually dismiss the Revolution of 1688–89 in England as a narrowly political event. They have argued that it was at most a political revolution, not a social revolution. They do so, however, because they have focused too narrowly on the constitutional achievements of 1689. The ideological contrast between Roger L'Estrange and John Locke reveals that there was much more at stake than a mere constitutional adjustment. The Revolution of 1688–89 transformed England from a pro-French into a pro-Dutch alignment. James II's government promoted an agrarian society; the postrevolutionary state adopted a political economy that favored manufacturing. The Church under James II was tightly controlled by high churchmen; after the revolution, it was dominated by a set of low church clergymen who were committed to religious toleration, monarchy limited by law, and social amelioration. The revolution radically altered the English state, the English economy, and the English church. The English had truly brought about the first modern revolution.

PART TWO

The Documents

The Revolution of 1688–1689

Most historical accounts of the Revolution of 1688–89 have focused on the dramatic events of October 1688 to February 1689. It was in these months that the regime of James II collapsed and William and Mary were declared king and queen. The revolution, it is widely held, was either an aristocratic coup d'état or a foreign conquest. The documents in this section explore both of these claims. What were the reasons William and his contemporaries offered for his risky Channel crossing in November 1688? What role did the English people play, if any, in the fall of the Stuart monarchy? How were contemporaries able to perceive and comprehend these momentous developments?

1

Invitation of the Seven to the Prince of Orange
June 30, 1688

As early as 1687, as William Prince of Orange contemplated the deteriorating political situation in England, he began to consider military intervention. He refused to act, however, without assurances of political support within England. A secret letter, signed by seven substantial noblemen in June 1688, played a critical role in convincing William that he had that support. The authorship of the letter was significant for William. Charles Talbot (Earl of Shrewsbury), William Cavendish (Earl of Devonshire), Henry Sidney, and Edward Russell were all Whigs, while Thomas Osborne (Earl of Danby), Richard Lumley (Lord Lumley), and Henry Compton (Bishop of London) were Tories. Devonshire, Danby, and Lumley all had power bases in the north of England. Sidney was influential in the army, while Russell had a great following in the navy. All of these men played significant roles in William's postrevolutionary regime.

Earl of Shrewsbury, Earl of Devonshire, Earl of Danby, Lord Lumley, Bishop Compton of London, Henry Sidney, and Edward Russell to Prince of Orange, June 30, 1688, Public Record Office, SP 8/1/Part II, ff. 224–27.

We have great reason to believe we shall be every day in a worse condition than we are, and less able to defend ourselves, and therefore we do earnestly wish we might be so happy as to find a remedy before it be too late for us to contribute to our own deliverance. . . . The people are so generally dissatisfied with the present conduct of the government in relation to their religion, liberties and properties (all which have been greatly invaded), and they are in such expectations of their prospects being daily worse, that your Highness may be assured there are nineteen parts of twenty of the people throughout the kingdom who are desirous of a change, and who we believe would willingly contribute to it if they had such a protection to countenance their rising, as could secure them from being destroyed before they could get to be in a posture able to defend themselves. . . . It is no less certain that much the greatest part of the nobility and gentry are as much dissatisfied, although it be not safe to speak to many of them beforehand. And there is no doubt but that some of the most considerable of them would venture themselves with your Highness at your first landing, whose interests would be able to draw great numbers to them whenever they could protect the raising and drawing men together. And if such a strength landed, as were able to defend itself and them till they could be got together into some order, we make no question but that strength would quickly be increased to double to the army here, although their army should remain firm to them. . . . Amongst the seamen it is almost certain, there is not one in ten who would do them any service in such a war. . . . We do upon very good grounds believe that [James II's] army would then be very much divided among themselves, many of the officers being so discontented that they continue in their service only for a subsistence (besides that some of their minds are known already) and very many of the common soldiers do daily show such an aversion to the popish religion that there is the greatest possibility imaginable of great numbers of deserters which would come from them should there be such an occasion. . . . Besides all this we do much doubt whether the present state of things will not yet be much changed to the worse before another year by a grand alteration, which will probably be made both in the officers and soldiers of the army, and by such other changes as are not only to be expected from a packed Parliament but what the meeting of any Parliament (in our present circumstances) may produce against those who will be looked upon as principal obstructers of their proceedings there, it being taken for granted that if things cannot then be carried to their wishes in a Parliamentary way, other measures will be put in execution by more violent means, and although such proceedings will then heighten the discontents, yet such courses will probably be taken at that time, as will prevent all possible means of relieving ourselves.

2

WILLIAM III

The Declaration
October 1688

William's Declaration *was written in the Dutch Republic by several hands. William collected a range of materials from English and Scottish exiles, as well as from his friends in England. The chief political officer of the province of Holland, Gaspar Fagel, drew up the document. Gilbert Burnet, the Scottish Church of England clergyman, translated the document into English and cleaned up the style. Thousands of copies of the* Declaration *were printed and smuggled into England in October and November 1688. Its contents were soon known throughout England and, indeed, throughout Europe.*

It is both certain and evident to all men that the public peace and happiness of any state or kingdom cannot be preserved where the laws, liberties and customs established, by the lawful authority in it, are openly transgressed and annulled; more especially where the alteration of religion is endeavored, and that a religion which is contrary to law is endeavored to be introduced, upon which those who are most immediately concerned in it, are indispensably bound to endeavor to preserve and maintain the established laws, liberties and customs, and above all the religion and worship of God that is established among them, and to take such an effectual care that the inhabitants of the said state or kingdom may neither be deprived of their religion, nor of their civil rights. Which is so much the more necessary because the greatness and security both of kings, royal families, and of all such as

William III, *The Declaration* (The Hague, [October] 1688).

are in authority, as well as the happiness of their subjects and people, depend, in a most especial manner, upon the exact observation and maintenance of these their laws, liberties and customs.

Upon these grounds it is that we cannot any longer forebear, to declare that, to our great regret, we see that those councilors, who have now the chief credit with the King, have overturned the religion, laws and liberties of those realms, and subjected them in all things relating to their consciences, liberties and properties, to arbitrary government, and that not only by secret and indirect ways, but in an open and undisguised manner....

It is also manifest and notorious that as His Majesty was, upon his coming to the crown, received and acknowledged by all the subjects of England, Scotland, and Ireland, as their King without the least opposition, though he made then open profession of the popish religion, so he did then promise and solemnly swear at his coronation that he would maintain his subjects in the free enjoyment of their laws, rights, liberties, and in particular, that he would maintain the Church of England as it was established by law. It is likewise certain that there have been, at diverse and sundry times, several laws enacted for the preservation of those rights, and liberties, and of the Protestant religion, and, among other securities, it has been enacted that all persons whatsoever that are advanced to any ecclesiastical dignity or to bear office in either university, as likewise all others that should be put in any employment, civil or military, should declare that they were not Papists, but were of the Protestant religion and that, by their taking of the oaths of allegiance and supremacy and the Test, yet these evil councilors have in effect annulled and abolished all those laws, both with relation to ecclesiastical and civil employment....

They have also invaded the privileges and seized on the charters of most of those towns that have a right to be represented by their burgesses in Parliament, and have procured surrenders to be made of them, by which the magistrates in them have delivered up all their rights and privileges to be disposed of at the pleasure of those evil councilors who have thereupon placed new magistrates in those towns, such as they can most entirely confide in. And in many of them, they have put popish magistrates, notwithstanding the incapacitates under which the law has put them....

Those great and insufferable oppressions and the open contempt of all law, together with the apprehensions of the sad consequences that must certainly follow upon it, have put the subjects under great and just fears, and have made them look after such lawful remedies as are allowed of in all nations. Yet, all has been without effect. And those evil councilors have endeavored to make all men apprehend the loss of their lives, liberties, honors, and estates, if they should go about to preserve themselves from this oppression by petitions, representations or other means authorized by law. . . .

And yet it cannot be pretended that any king, how great so ever their power has been, and how arbitrary and despotic so ever they have been in the exercise of it, have ever reckoned it a crime for their subjects to come in all submission and respect, and in a due number not exceeding the limits of the law, and represent to them the reasons that make it impossible for them to obey their orders. . . .

The last and great remedy for all those evils is the calling of a Parliament, for securing the nation against the evil practices of those wicked councilors, but this could not be yet compassed, nor can it be easily brought about. For those men, apprehending that a lawful Parliament, being once assembled, they would be brought to an account for all their open violations of law and for their plots and conspiracies against the Protestant religion, and the lives and liberties of the subjects, they have endeavored under the specious pretense of liberty of conscience: first, to sow divisions among Protestants, between those of the Church of England and the Dissenters, the design being laid to engage Protestants that are all equally concerned to preserve themselves from popish oppression into mutual quarreling, that so by this some advantage might be given to them to bring about their designs, and that both in the election of the members of Parliament, and afterwards in the Parliament itself. For they see well that if all Protestants could enter into a mutual good understanding one with another, and concur together in the preserving of their religion, it would not be possible for them to compass their wicked ends. They have also required all persons in the several counties of England that either were in any employment, or were in any considerable esteem to declare beforehand, that they would concur in the repeal of the Test and Penal laws, and that they would give their voices in the elections to Parliament, only for such as would concur in it. Such as would not thus pre-engage themselves were turned out of all employments, and others who entered into those engagements were put in their places, many of them being Papists. And, contrary to the charters and privileges of those boroughs that have a right to send burgesses to Parliament, they have ordered such regulations to be made, as they thought fit and necessary, for assuring themselves of all the members that are to be chosen by those corporations, and by this means they hope to avoid that punishment which they have deserved, though it is apparent that all acts made by popish magistrates are null and void of themselves, so sheriffs and mayors of towns; and therefore, as long as the authority and magistracy is in such hands it is not possible to have any lawful Parliament. And though according to the Constitution of the English government and immemorial custom, all elections of Parliament men ought to be made with an entire liberty without any sort of force, or the requiring the electors to choose such persons as shall be named to them, and the persons thus freely elected ought to give their opinions freely upon all matters that are brought before them, having the good of the nation ever before their eyes and following in all things the dictates of their conscience, yet now the people of England cannot expect a remedy from a free Parliament, legally called and chosen. But they may perhaps see one called in which all elections will be carried by fraud or force, and which will be composed of such persons, of whom those evil councilors hold themselves assured, in which all things will be carried on according to their direction and interest, without any regard to the good or happiness of the nation. . . .

Therefore, it is, that we have thought fit to go over to England, and to carry over with us a force sufficient by the blessing of God to defend us from the violence of those evil councilors. And we, being desirous that our intentions in this may be rightly understood, have for this end prepared this declaration in which, as we have hitherto given a true account of the reasons inducing us to it, so we now think it fit to declare that this our expedition is intended for no other design but to have a free and lawful Parliament assembled as soon as is possible, and that in order to this, all the later charters by which the elections of burgesses are limited contrary to the ancient custom shall be considered as null and of no force, and employments, as well as the boroughs of England, shall return again to their ancient prescriptions and charters; and more particularly that the ancient charter of the great and famous city of London, shall again be in force, and that the writs for the members of Parliament shall be addressed to the proper officers, according to law and custom. That also none be suffered to choose or be chosen members of Parliament but such as are qualified by law, and that the members of Parliament, being thus lawfully chosen, they shall meet and sit in full freedom, that so the two houses may concur in the preparing of such laws as they upon the law concerning the Test and such other laws as are necessary for the security and maintenance of the Protestant religion, as likewise for making such law as may establish a good agreement between the Church of

England, and all Protestant Dissenters, as also for the covering and securing of all such who will live peaceably under the government, as becomes good subjects, from all persecution upon the account of their religion, even Papists themselves not excepted, and for the doing of all things which the two houses of Parliament shall find necessary for the peace, honor and safety of the nation, so that there may be no more danger of the nations falling at any time hereafter under arbitrary government. . . .

And we for our part will concur in everything that may procure the peace and happiness of that nation, which a free and lawful Parliament shall determine, since we have nothing before our eyes in this our undertaking but the preservation of the Protestant religion, the covering of all men from persecution for their conscience, and the securing to the whole nation the free enjoyment of all their laws, rights, and liberties, under a just and legal government.

This is the design that we have proposed to ourselves in appearing upon this occasion in arms, in the conduct of which we will keep the forces under our command, under all the strictness of martial discipline, and take a special care that the people of the countries through which we must march shall not suffer by their means; and as soon as the state of the nation will admit of it, we promise that we will send back all those foreign forces that we have brought along with us.

We do therefore hope that all people will judge rightly of us and approve of these our proceedings, but we chiefly rely on the blessing of God for the success of this our undertaking, in which we place our whole and only confidence.

We do, in the last place, invite and require all persons whatsoever, all the peers of the realm, both spiritual and temporal, all Lords Lieutenants, deputy Lieutenants, and all gentlemen, citizens and other commons of all ranks to come and assist us in order to the executing this our design against all such as shall endeavor to oppose us; that so we may prevent all those miseries, which must needs follow upon the nations being kept under arbitrary government and slavery, and that all the violence and disorders which have overturned the whole Constitution of the English government may be fully redressed in a free and legal Parliament. . . .

3

FRANCIS BARRINGTON AND BENJAMIN STEELE

A Letter Describing the Revolution to Thomas Goodwin and Kinnard Delabere

January 11, 1689

The authors of the letter excerpted here were merchants who traded currants, cloths, and oils in the Mediterranean. Based in London, they had to keep their Tunis-based trading partners informed about everything that could affect their business concerns, including the events of the Revolution of 1688–89.

And now we come to give you a relation of what public transactions have lately passed in England. On the 5th November the Prince of Orange landed his army at Torbay and Dartmouth and Exmouth, according to computation being about 10,000 foot and 3,500 horse besides gentlemen volunteers. With these he marches to Exeter which city received him with acclamations. There he stayed about a fortnight, recruited his wearied men, but much more disabled horses. The King's forces rendezvoused at Salisbury and was the completest army, perhaps, in the world, their numbers considered. For 'tis judged they were not above 20,000 foot and 8,000 horse. The Prince beginning his march towards the King's army, my Lord Cornbury[1] with three entire regiments of horse made the first defection from Salisbury, going directly to deliver themselves to the Prince's protection. Thereupon the generality of the nobility went to the Prince and in association gave themselves into his protection. Upon this the King leaves London and goes to his army to settle their minds. But then happened worser mischief to him. For in one night deserted him my Lord Churchill[2]

---

[1] Edward Hyde, Lord Cornbury (1661–1724), the first officer of rank to desert James II and to deliver his forces to the Prince of Orange.

[2] John Churchill, Lord Marlborough (1650–1722), a longtime friend and confidant of James II.

Francis Barrington and Benjamin Steele (London) to Thomas Goodwin and Kinnard Delabere, January 11, 1689, Public Record Office, FO 335/8/3.

(who was a lieutenant general of the army), the Duke of Ormond,[3] the Duke of Grafton,[4] &c. A short time after [the] Prince of Denmark[5] deserted him and the Princess Anne.[6] My Lord Delamere,[7] my Lord Danby,[8] my Lord Devonshire[9] and many others raise the several counties declaring for the Prince of Orange; in fine a universal defection throughout the nation of nobility, gentry and commonalty. This so startled his Majesty that he first ships off his Queen and the Prince of Wales for France and the next night privately went by water himself. But by the fishermen of Feversham in Kent he was seized; and a few days after he returned to Whitehall. The Prince being then near London sent the night before he arrived to dismount the King's guards about Whitehall and mount his own in their rooms. Upon this the King the next morning by barge went to Rochester and continued there some few days not under any constraint; but imagining (as 'tis supposed) somewhat worse might follow he embarks a second time for France and thither he arrived in safety. The present administration of the government is by the nobility and gentry involved (for the present) by the Prince of Orange and a Parliament called to settle things in some better posture who are to meet on the 22nd of this instant.

Now certainly when the providences of God are considered in this whole transaction, never anything happened with so many amazing circumstances as this hath done—the bonding of the spirits of people so universally one way, nay even the minds of persons whose long differings with each other made one think 'twas impossible they should be reconciled in anything, did all agree to help on this work; the speediness of its execution; and all without the loss of 50 men on all sides—makes it the most astonishing alteration that ever yet befell any one part of the universe. . . .

---

[3]James Butler, 2nd Duke of Ormonde (1665–1745).
[4]Henry Fitzroy, 1st Duke of Grafton (1663–1690), second illegitimate son of Charles II.
[5]Prince George of Denmark (1653–1708), consort of Queen Anne, whom he married in 1683.
[6]Anne, Queen of Great Britain and Ireland (1665–1714), the younger daughter of James II and his first wife, Anne Hyde. She succeeded her brother-in-law, William, in 1702 and reigned until her death in 1714.
[7]Henry Booth, Lord Delamere (1652–1694), a zealous Whig.
[8]Thomas Osborne, 1st Earl of Danby (1632–1712), a Tory.
[9]William Cavendish, 4th Earl of Devonshire (1640–1707), a Whig.

4

LORD DELAMERE

Reasons Why the King Ran Away

1690s

Lord Delamere (1652–1694), the author of this essay, which explains the king's flight from Salisbury, was a committed Whig politician. Though his father had taken up arms in favor of restoring the monarchy in the 1650s, Delamere was increasingly disenchanted with the rule of Charles II and James II. In November 1688, he personally led a rising in Cheshire that linked up with the forces of the Duke of Devonshire at Nottingham, after marching through Derbyshire. Delamere, though himself a member of the Church of England, had a large following among Presbyterians.

And with like steps they moved at Nottingham, and other places: And though no doubt they engaged in the business with a great deal of zeal and resolution, yet the declaration of the cause of their assembling, was penned with great caution, perhaps as a considerable man amongst them said, to keep themselves within the statute; for their declaration, neither charged King James with mal-administration, nor complained of the danger we were in, but the sum of it was to join with the Prince of Orange in declaring for a free Parliament: whereby they put it into King James his power to oblige them to put up their swords as soon as he pleased; for when ever he issued out his proclamation for a free Parliament, they were bound in honour to lay down their arms: And then what very great service can they boast of who could hold swords in their hand no longer than King James from having a true account of their numbers, and as they would daily increase, so every account he had of them would make them still more considerable. They showed thereby, that they were resolved not to look back, but would either conquer or die. They did not mince the matter,

---

Lord Delamere, *The Works of the Right Honourable Henry Late L. Delamer, and Earl of Warrington: Containing His Lordship's Advice to His Children, Several Speeches in Parliament* (London, 1694), 67–69.

but spoke plain English of King James, and of our condition, and thereby animated the country as they marched, and made all sure behind them, so that the further they marched the greater service they did, for 500 men thus moving would in a short time occasion 40,000 to rise in arms; whereby in a few days they would not only be reported, but in effect be so considerable and formidable as to support the cause they had espoused, and either reduce King James to measures, or drive him out of the kingdom: So that this seems to be the great thing that so astonished King James, and put him to his wits' ends. For as to the Prince's forces, their number was not valuable, and if pressed very hard would not too obstinately stand it out, because it was evident they had a retreat in their thoughts, and accordingly had provided for it. The desertion in his army he could not much regard, because it did not amount to 2,000 men, till he ran away: But as to those who intended to join with the Prince of Orange his army; he would with dread behold the storm coming upon him, for he might observe the cloud no bigger at first than a man's hand, increased so fast, that it would quickly over spread the whole heavens, and prove so great a weight, that it would bear down all before it; for their numbers would quickly swell very high, and it could not be foreseen, where and at what degree they would stop: He might plainly see, that they had thrown away the scabbard, and contemned the thoughts of asking quarter; for as they could never hope for another opportunity to recover their liberties if they failed in this, so they very well knew the inexorable temper of King James, that it would be to no great purpose to sue for his mercy; whereby being made desperate, and abetted moreover by the whole nation; he must expect the utmost that could be done by the united vigor of courage, revenge, the recovery of liberty, and despair, all which would make up too strong a composition for King James his tender stomach, and turn his thoughts from fighting, to contrive the best way to save his life, and this was the storm that drove him away from Salisbury.

5

COLLEY CIBBER

Memoir of the Revolution
1740

Colley Cibber (1671–1757) was an important actor, dramatist, and literary critic in the eighteenth century. In 1688, he was a young man, already with deep Whig sympathies. He took up arms with the Earl of Devonshire at Nottingham, as he relates in this excerpt from his autobiography. Cibber's father, a prominent stonemason, was then working on the Earl of Devonshire's house at Chatsworth.

Before I could set out on my journey [to Cambridge], the nation fell in labor of the revolution, the news being then just brought to London that the Prince of Orange at the head of an army was landed in the West. When I came to Nottingham, I found my father in arms there, among those forces which the Earl of Devonshire had raised for the redress of our violated laws and liberties. . . .

You must now consider me as one among those desperate thousands, who, after a patience sorely tried, took arms under the banner of necessity, the natural parent of all human laws and government. I question if in all the histories of empire there is one instance of so bloodless a revolution as that in England in 1688, wherein Whigs, Tories, princes, prelates, nobles, clergy, common people, and a standing army, were unanimous. To have seen all England of one mind is to have lived at a very particular juncture. Happy nation who are never divided among themselves but when they have least to complain of! Our greatest grievance since that time seems to have been that we cannot all govern; and 'till the number of good places are equal to those who think themselves qualified for them there must ever be a cause of contention among us. . . .

It were almost incredible to tell you, at the latter end of King James's time (though the rod of arbitrary power was always shaking

Colley Cibber, *An Apology for the Life of Mr. Colley Cibber, Comedian, and Late Patentee of the Theatre-Royal,* 2nd ed. (London: John Watts, 1740), 60–63.

over us) with what freedom and contempt the common people in the open streets talked of his wild measures to make a whole Protestant nation Papists; and yet, in the height of our secure and wanton defiance of him, we of the vulgar had no farther notion of any remedy for this evil than a satisfied presumption that our numbers were too great to be mastered by his mere will and pleasure; that though he might be too hard for our laws, he would never be able to get the better of our nature; and that to drive all England into popery and slavery he would find would be teaching an old lion to dance.

But happy it was for the nation that it had then wiser heads in it, who knew how to lead a people so disposed into measures for the public preservation. . . .

If [James I, Charles I, Charles II, and James II] had exercised their regal authority with so visible a regard to the public welfare [as Queen Elizabeth I], it were hard to know whether the people of England might have ever complained of them, or even felt the want of that liberty they now so happily enjoy. 'Tis true that before [Elizabeth's] time our ancestors had many successful contests with their sovereigns for their ancient right and claim to it; yet what did those successes amount to? Little more than a declaration that there was such a right in being; but who ever saw it enjoyed? Did not the actions of almost every succeeding reign show there were still so many doors of oppression left open to prerogative that (whatever value our most eloquent legislators may have set upon those ancient liberties) I doubt it will be difficult to fix the period of their having a real being before the revolution: or if there ever was an elder period of our unmolested enjoying them, I own my poor judgment is at a loss where to place it. I will boldly say then, it is to the revolution only we owe the full possession of what, 'till then, we never had more than a perpetually contested right to: and, from thence, from the revolution it is that the Protestant successors of King William have found their paternal care and maintenance of that right has been the surest basis of their glory.

The Eighteenth-Century Debate

Although the causes, consequences, and significance of the Revolution of 1688–89 were contested almost from the outset, the debate over the revolution rose to new heights in the late eighteenth century.

At that time, many in England sought to compare their Revolution of 1688–89 with the revolution breaking out in France in 1789. Richard Price and Edmund Burke made two of the most significant contributions to that debate. Most subsequent historians have followed Burke in contrasting the Revolution of 1688–89 with subsequent revolutions.

6

RICHARD PRICE

A Celebration of the Revolution of 1688–1689
November 4, 1789

Richard Price (1723–1791) was an extremely influential political radical and Nonconformist cleric. He delivered a sermon to the Revolution Society of London, a group dedicated to celebrating the Revolution Principles of 1688–89. The sermon, excerpted here, sparked off a controversy over the meaning of the revolution and provoked many newly formed Revolution Clubs in France to voice their admiration for England's revolution. It also provoked a number of angry responses within the British Isles.

Civil government (as I have before observed) is an institution of human prudence for guarding our persons, our property, and our good name, against invasion; and for securing to the members of a community that liberty to which all have an equal right as far as they do not, by any overt act, use it to injure the liberty of others. Civil laws are regulations agreed upon by the community for gaining these ends; and civil magistrates are officers appointed by the community for executing these laws. Obedience, therefore, to the laws and to magistrates, is a necessary expression of our regard to the community. Without it a community must fall into a state of anarchy that will destroy those

Richard Price, *A Discourse on the Love of Our Country Delivered on Nov. 4, 1789, at the Meeting-House in the Old Jewry, to the Society for Commemorating the Revolution in Great Britain* (London: T. Cadell, 1790), 20–25, 31–39.

rights and subvert that liberty, which it is the end of government to protect. . . .

We are met to thank God for that event in this country to which the name of the Revolution has been given; and which, for more than a century, it has been usual for the friends of freedom, and more especially Protestant Dissenters, to celebrate with expressions of joy and exultation. . . . By a bloodless victory, the fetters which despotism had been long preparing for us were broken; the rights of the people were asserted, a tyrant expelled, and a sovereign of our own choice appointed in his room. Security was given to our property, and our consciences were emancipated. The bounds of free enquiry were enlarged; the volume in which are the words of eternal life, was laid more open to our examination; and that era of light and liberty was introduced among us, by which we have been made an example to other kingdoms, and became the instructors of the world. Had it not been for this deliverance, the probability is, that instead of being thus distinguished, we should now have been a base people, groaning under the infamy and misery of popery and slavery. . . .

It is well known that King James was not far from gaining his purpose; and that probably he would have succeeded, had he been less in a hurry. But he wanted courage as well as prudence; and, therefore, fled, and left us to settle quietly for ourselves that constitution of government which is now our boast. We have particular reason, as Protestant Dissenters, to rejoice on this occasion. It was at this time we were rescued from persecution and obtained the liberty of worshipping God in the manner we think most acceptable to him. It was then our meeting houses we opened, our worship was taken under the protection of the law, and the principles of toleration gained a triumph. We have, therefore, on this occasion peculiar reasons for thanksgivings. Our gratitude, if genuine, will be accompanied with endeavors to give stability to the deliverance our country had obtained, and to extend and improve the happiness with which the Revolution has blest us—let us, in particular, take care not to forget the principles of the Revolution. This Society, has, very properly, in its reports, held out these principles, as an instruction to the public. I will only take notice of the three following:

First, the right to liberty of conscience in religious matters.

Secondly, the right to resist power when abused. And,

Thirdly, the right to choose our own governors; to cashier them for misconduct; and to frame a government for ourselves.

On these three principles, and more especially the last, was the

Revolution founded. Were it not true that liberty of conscience is a sacred right; that power abused justifies resistance, and the civil authority is a delegation from the people—Were not, I say, all this true; the Revolution would have been not an assertion, but an invasion of rights; not a revolution, but a rebellion. Cherish in your own breasts this conviction, and act under its influence; detesting the odious doctrines of passive obedience, nonresistance, and the divine right of kings—doctrines which, had they been acted upon in this country, would have left us at this time wretched slaves—doctrines which imply, that God made mankind to be oppressed and plundered; and which are no less a blasphemy against him, than an insult on common sense.

7

EDMUND BURKE

The Significance of the Revolution of 1688–1689

1790

Edmund Burke (1729–1797) was one of the great statesmen of late-eighteenth-century Britain. During his long political career, his parliamentary speeches, legal arguments, and political pamphlets marked him as one of the great stylists and political thinkers of his age. Although Burke was a Whig, the widely circulated pamphlet excerpted here was deeply influential among the opponents of the French Revolution. He offered an interpretation of the events of 1688–89 that accorded neither with Price's view of the Revolution Principles nor with Jacobite defenses of the cause of James II.

On the forenoon of the 4th of November last, Dr. Richard Price, a nonconforming minister of eminence, preached at the dissenting meeting-house of the Old Jewry, to his club or society, a very extraordinary

Edmund Burke, *Reflections on the Revolution in France* (London, 1790), 12–14, 21–24, 29–32, 44–45.

miscellaneous sermon, in which there are some good moral and religious sentiments, and not ill expressed, mixed up in a sort of porridge of various political opinions and reflections. . . .

This pulpit style, revived after so long a discontinuance, had to me the air of novelty, and of a novelty not wholly without danger. . . .

If the principles of the Revolution of 1688 are anywhere to be found, it is in the statute called the *Declaration of Right.* In that most wise, sober, and considerate declaration, drawn up by great lawyers and great statesmen, and not by warm and inexperienced enthusiasts, not one word is said, nor one suggestion made, of a general right "to choose our own governors; to cashier them for misconduct; and to form a government of ourselves."

This Declaration of Right (the act of the 1st of William and Mary, sess. 2. ch. 2.) is the cornerstone of our constitution, as reinforced, explained, improved, and in its fundamental principles forever settled. It is called "An act for declaring the rights and liberties of the subject and for settling the succession of the crown." You will observe, that these rights and this succession are declared in one body, and bound indissolubly together. . . .

Unquestionably there was at the Revolution, in the person of King William, a small and a temporary deviation from the strict order of a regular hereditary succession; but it is against all genuine principles of jurisprudence to draw a principle from law made in a special case, and regarding an individual person. . . . If ever there was a time favorable for establishing a principle, that a king of popular choice was the only legal king, without all doubt it was at the Revolution. Its not being done at this time is a proof that the nation was of opinion it ought not to be done at any time. There is no person so completely ignorant of our history, as not to know, that the majority in the parliament of both parties were so little disposed to any thing resembling that principle, that at first they were determined to place the vacant crown, not on the head of the Prince of Orange, but on that of his wife Mary, daughter of King James, the eldest born of the issue of that King, which they acknowledged as undoubtedly his. It would be to repeat a very trite story, to recall to your memory all those circumstances which demonstrated that their accepting King William was not properly a choice; but, to all those who did not wish, in effect to recall King James, or to deluge their country in blood, and again to bring their religion, laws, and liberties into the peril they had just escaped, it was an act of necessity, in the strictest moral sense in which necessity can be taken. . . .

The gentlemen of the Society for Revolutions see nothing in that of 1688 but the deviation from the constitution; and they take the deviation from the principle for the principle. They have little regard to the obvious consequences of their doctrine, though they must see, that it leaves positive authority in very few of the positive institutions of this country. When such an unwarrantable maxim is once established, that no throne is lawful but the elective, no one act of the princes who preceded their era of fictitious election can be valid. Do these theorists mean to imitate some of their predecessors who dragged the bodies of our ancient sovereigns out of the quiet of their tombs? Do they mean to attaint and disable backwards all the kings that have reigned before the Revolution, and consequently to stain the throne of England with the blot of continual usurpation? Do they mean to invalidate, annul, or to call into question, together with the titles of the whole line of our kings, that great body of our statute law which passed under those whom they treat as usurpers? To annul laws of inestimable value to our liberties—of as great value at least as any which have passed at or since the period of the Revolution? . . .

The Revolution was made to preserve our ancient indisputable laws and liberties, and that ancient constitution of government which is our only security for law and liberty. If you are desirous of knowing the spirit of our constitution, and the policy which predominated in that great period which has secured it to this hour, pray look for both in our histories, in our records, in our acts of parliament, and journals of parliament, and not in the sermons of the Old Jewry, and after-dinner toasts of the Revolution Society.—In the former you will find other ideas and another language. Such a claim is as ill-suited to our temper and wishes as it is unsupported by any appearance of authority. The very idea of the fabrication of a new government, is enough to fill us with disgust and horror. We wished at the period of the Revolution, and do now wish, to derive all we possess as an inheritance from our forefathers. Upon that body and stock of inheritance we have taken care not to inoculate any scion alien to the nature of the original plant. All the reformations we have hitherto made, have proceeded upon the principle of reference to antiquity; and I hope, nay I am persuaded, that all those which possibly may be made hereafter, will be carefully formed upon analogical precedent, authority, and example.

Social and Economic Background

The history of England's economy and society in the late seventeenth century has traditionally been neglected. Focusing their energies on the economic context of the outbreak of the civil wars (1642–47) or on the origins of the industrial revolution, historians have treated the intervening age somewhat condescendingly as a period of modest growth but no significant developments. Recent comparative work by economists, however, is prompting a reassessment of the economy of the late seventeenth century. England's modest growth was remarkable in the context of a Europe beset by economic crisis. Only the Dutch Republic and England possessed thriving economies between 1650 and 1700. Indeed, the dramatic political revolution of 1688–89 may have been but the most visible of transformations in an England undergoing pronounced urbanization and commercialization. Together, these documents suggest the ways in which the court and the broader reading public perceived those changes. They also suggest some of the new social institutions that emerged between 1650 and 1700 that transformed the daily lives of English men and women.

8

The Growing Social and Political Importance of Foreign Trade

1685

The anonymous memorandum excerpted here was drawn up and circulated among James II's political inner circle almost immediately after he came to the throne. It may well have been written by one of James II's fellow members of the Royal African Company. Its existence suggests how important issues of political economy were to the government of James II.

"An Essay on the Interest of the Crown in American Plantations," British Library, Add. MSS 47131, ff. 24–25.

Trade and negotiation has infected the whole kingdom, and no man disdains to marry or mix with it. By this means the very genius of the people is altered, and it will in the end be the interest of the crown to proportion its maxims of power suitable to this new nature come among us. . . . It should be considered that trade is a natural emanation of the mind's freedom, every man being left to his own choice in a manner, from what part of the world to raise his revenues by it, so that it infects by degrees their heads with popular and republican notions, and makes them ever inclined to be improvers of discourses and designs which tend that way, every man having a kind of sanctuary in his pate [head] to which he means to retire should there happen to be civil broils. This causes that eternal noise and wild manner of talk in city coffeehouses, where you shall hear one man contending for the interest of Holland and another for Hamburg, a third for Spain, another for Venice and so on, till Turkey itself appears the happiest place in the world in some of their opinions, that truly to hear their arguments, a stranger might very well believe there was not one Englishman in the room, and this as men's conversations lie sets the whole people agog to think felicity is to be had in every country but this, and no wonder then if they love the government accordingly. . . . To remedy these inconveniences and to place the monarchy on its right basis would be to mix the interest of the crown and the overbalance of the kingdom[10] together, as it was when land supported the whole and that our kings had every third acre their own, whereas, by degrees, having distributed that fund of power, no care has been taken to settle any other in its stead. So that every succeeding king on his accession to the crown must be forced to command hard and questionable things, or hold his title and power precariously at the will and pleasure of some popular prevailing faction, besides the inconvenience of never being able to embark the interest of the nation in a necessary foreign war. Moreover, the support of the crown as it is now settled, seeming to be a pension from the people, makes them insolent and saucy in their discourses of the Prince's actions and alliances, impudently pretending to have a right to direct the spending of that they think they give.

[10]The trading sector.

9

GUY MIEGE

Social Life in Late-Seventeenth-Century England

1691

Guy Miege was a Swiss Protestant immigrant to England in the late seventeenth century. His descriptions of England went through almost yearly editions well into the eighteenth century. His New State of England *was purchased and read throughout England and was widely consulted by continental visitors as well. Miege's narrative was based on personal observation—he traveled the length and breadth of England several times—as well as on printed accounts. The text provided natives and foreigners alike with much basic information, from the names of England's rivers to the structure of the judicial system.*

When all is done, I have this to urge in the behalf of great cities, that they are a visible sign of a flourishing state, and such as draws respect from its neighbors, who look upon it as the luxuriance and result of its wealth. And, of all the cities of Europe, none can so justly challenge the pre-eminency in this point as London, the metropolis of England; being not only perhaps the most ancient, but also the wealthiest, and (reckoning all its annexes) the greatest city now extant in Europe.

Such a city as contains above 600 streets, lanes, courts, and alleys; and in them all, by a late computation, at least a hundred thousand houses. So that, allowing only 8 persons to each house one with another (which I think is moderate), the number of the inhabitants will amount at that rate to above eight hundred thousand souls. Besides a world of seamen, that live and swarm in that constant (though moving) forest of ships down the river, on the east side of the bridge.

The dwelling houses raised since the fire[11] are generally very fair,

---

[11]The Great Fire of London, in September 1666, destroyed St. Paul's Cathedral, the Guildhall, the Royal Exchange, eighty-seven parish churches, and more than thirteen thousand houses.

Guy Miege, *The New State of England under Their Majesties K. William and Q. Mary* (London: H. C. for John Wyat, 1691), part 1, 281–85, 335–39; part 2, 31–38, 46–49, 55–58.

and built much more convenient and uniform than heretofore. Before the fire, they were most timber-houses, built with little regard to uniformity; but since the fire, building of bricks has been the general way, and that with so much art and skill in architecture, that I have often wondered to see in well-compact houses so many conveniences in a small compass of ground. In short, our English builders have built so much of late years, that no nation perhaps at this time can vie with them for making much of any ground (though never so little) and contriving all the parts of it to the best advantage, in the neatest and most regular way, with all the conveniences the ground can possibly afford. . . .

If we come to stateliness, I confess the noblemen's houses at Paris, being built of free stone (as most of that city are) with large courts before 'em for the reception of coaches, make a fine outward appearance. But, for uniformity, state, and magnificence, we have some here, and chiefly Montague House, that exceed by far most of 'em. As for great merchants' houses, and fair taverns, scarce any city surpasses London in this particular. For public buildings, as halls, Inns of Court, exchanges, market-places, hospitals, colleges, churches, besides the Bridge upon the river, the Monument, Custom-House, and the Tower, they are things worth any stranger's curiosity to view, at least a good part of them. Most of which have indeed the disadvantage of being built backward, and out of the way, to make room for tradesmen's shops in the streets. Whereas, if they had been all built towards the street, as generally they are in other countries, few cities could make so great an appearance. . . .

Lastly, when I reflect upon that dismal fire, which in three days' time consumed above thirteen thousand Houses (besides 89 parish-churches, the vast cathedral of St. Paul, diverse chapels, halls, colleges, schools, and other public edifices), it is a matter of amazement to me to see how soon the English recovered themselves from so great a desolation, and a loss not to be computed. At 3 years end near upon ten thousand houses were raised up again from their ashes, with great improvements. And by that time the fit of building grew so strong, that, besides a full and glorious restoration of a city that a raging fire had lately buried in its ashes, the suburbs have been increased to that degree, that (to speak modestly) as many more houses have been added to it, with all the advantages that able and skilful builders could invent, both for conveniency and beauty. . . .

I conclude, as to London, with three notable conveniences it has, not elsewhere to be found; viz. the New Lights, the Penny-Post, and the Insurance-Office for houses in case of fire.

The New Lights is so ingenious and useful an invention, that Mr. Edmund Heming the inventor deserves an immortal praise for it. He brought it to light about 6 years ago, with a patent from King Charles II, for the enjoyment of the profits thereof. And such is the reflection of these lights, though at a good distance from each other, that few of them serve to light a whole street in the night, better than ten times the number of glass lanterns. For, by the regular position of one of them before the front of every tenth house on each side of a broad street, there is such a mutual reflection, that they all seem to be but one great solar light. . . .

The Penny-Post is such a contrivance, that for one penny a letter, or parcel not exceeding one pound weight, or ten pounds in value, is presently conveyed from all parts of the town and suburbs to the remotest places thereof. And it has been so far improved, since the first settling of it, as to reach ten miles about London. He that sends pays the penny; and, when the letter or parcel goes beyond the bounds of the weekly Bills of Mortality,[12] the receiver pays another Penny. . . .

The Insurance Office for houses in case of fire is also an invention worth our taking notice. To insure, for example, 100 £. upon a brick house, the rates are 6 shillings for one Year, 12 for two years, 18 for three Years; and double for a timber-house. But, if any insure for four years, there is a discount allowed for paying down the money, so that he pays but three years and a quarter; and proportionably five for seven, seven for eleven years insurance. And, as often as the house is burnt, or demolished by reason of fire, within the term insured, the money insured on the house is to be paid; but, if only damaged, then to be repaired at the charge of the office. For the security of which payment, the office has a fund to the value of 60,000 £. in ground-Rents of inheritance (which is above 2,600 £. per annum) to answer losses and damages; and settled on twelve gentlemen trustees, by many of the most eminent counsel at law.

This ingenious and useful invention was first put into practice about 8 years since, and has deservedly met with good encouragement, insomuch that there are now above 7,300 houses insured. The office is kept on the back-side of the Royal-Exchange, and at the Rainbow Coffee-house by the Inner-Temple Gate at Fleet Street.

Now, to put a present stop, as far as is possible, to any sudden fire, there are belonging to the office a great many stout and lusty servants

---

[12]Beyond the boundary of greater London.

in livery with badges, dwelling in several parts of the city, and always to be ready on all occasions of sudden fires. Who, in such cases, do commonly expose themselves to the utmost hazards, and with great dexterity labor to suppress the fire. . . .

When I compare the modern English way of building with the old way, I cannot but wonder at the genius of old times. Nothing is more delightful and convenient than light, nothing more agreeable to health than a free air. And yet of old they used to dwell in houses, most with a blind staircase, low ceilings, and dark windows; the rooms built at random, often with steps from one to another. So that one would think the men of former ages were afraid of light and good air, or loved to play at hide and seek. Whereas the genius of our time is altogether for lightsome staircases, fine sash-windows, and lofty ceilings. And such has been of late our builders' industry, in point of compactness and uniformity, that a house after the new way will afford upon the same quantity of ground as many more conveniences.

The contrivance of closets in most rooms, and the painted wainscoting now so much used, are also two great improvements, the one for conveniency, the other for cleanness and health. And indeed, for so damp a country as England is, nothing could be better contrived than wainscot, to keep off the ill impression of damp walls. In short, for handsome accommodations and neatness of lodgings, London undoubtedly has got the preeminence.

The greatest objection against the London houses (being for the most part brick) is their Slightness, occasioned by the fines exacted by the landlords. So that few houses, at the common rate of building, last longer than the ground-lease, that is about 50 or 60 years. In the mean time, if there happens to be a long fit of excessive heat in summer or cold in winter, the walls being but thin, become at last so penetrated with the air, that the tenant must needs be uneasy with it. But those extremes happen but seldom. And this way of building is wonderful beneficial to all trades relating to it; for they never want work in so great a city, where houses here and there are always repairing, or building up again.

The plastered ceilings, so much used in England beyond all other countries, make by their whiteness the rooms so much lightsomer, and are excellent against a raging fire. They stop the passage of dust, and lessen the noise overhead. In summertime the air of the room is something the cooler for it, and the warmer in winter.

The use of stoves, so common in northern countries, as Germany, Denmark, Sweden, Poland, and Moscovy, and even so far southward as Switzerland, is in a manner unknown in this country. And indeed its temperateness does no way require it. Therefore the English use no outward remedy against cold weather but chimney-fire, which is both comfortable to the body, and cheerful to the sight. 'Tis true, there is a double conveniency in stoves. First in point of savings, for once heating of a stove in the morning, keeps the room warm a whole day. Secondly, in point of warmth, the room being so warm with it, that all places in it feel the benefit thereof. But those two conveniences are more than over-balanced to gather and foment all the noisome smells of a room for want of vent, which must needs be very unwholesome; whereas a chimney-fire draws 'em to it, and there they find vent with the smoke. To that inconveniency we may add the chilling impressions of a cold and sharp air, upon ones coming into it out of so warm a room as commonly stove-rooms are. Besides the cumbersomeness of stoves in summertime, when being altogether useless, they take up a great deal of room to no purpose.

As for fuel, England affords three sorts, wood, coals, and turves;[13] but coals is the most common, in London especially, where they have 'em by sea from Newcastle and Sunderland. A lasting sort of fuel, being a mixture of small and round coals together, which by their aptness to cake, is the most durable of any; and for kitchen use, far beyond wood itself, as yielding not only a more even, but more piercing heat. The smoke of it is indeed grosser, and of a corrosive nature; but yet nothing so offensive to the eye, whatever it is to the lungs, as some pretend it to be. In many parts of the country they have pit-coals, which is a cleaner and more cheerful fuel, but not so durable as sea-coals. But the cheapness of these at London in time of peace is worth taking notice; where for so small a matter as two or three pence a day one may keep a constant moderate fire from morning till bedtime. Which is a mighty advantage to so vast and populous a place, especially considering it comes 300 miles by sea. And whatever the Parisians can say to the praise of their wood fires, I dare say the common sort of people there would be glad, could they compass it, to change in wintertime fuel with the Londoners.

The English diet falls next under our consideration; which for the eating part, does most consist in flesh, and chiefly in butcher's meat. For, though they have great plenty and variety of fish and fowl, roots and herbs, yet they are most commonly used but as a supplement or an accessory to the principal. And therefore the English ever went

[13]Slabs of peat used for fuel. *Turves* is the plural of *turf.*

amongst the strangers for the greatest flesh-eaters. Which is certainly the best, and the most proper nourishment for this country.

But, whereas formerly the English used to eat three or four meals a day, the generality of them, since the long Civil Wars in this reign of Charles I have used themselves to eat but one meal a day. If then they eat plentifully, and perhaps beyond the rate of other people, who eat three or four times a day, it is no matter of amazement. Some thing more than ordinary must be laid up in store, to hold out 24 hours. There is the less time lost in eating, and the more favored for business. So that, if other nations live to eat, the English may be said to eat only to live. In short, all things considered, we may reckon the English, (who heretofore were perhaps not unjustly taxed of gluttony, and to be a people most given to their bellies) to be now one of the most sober nations of Europe, as to eating. . . .

But the Civil Wars aforesaid are not the only thing which has brought the English to this moderation of eating but one meal a day. The frequent use of tobacco, tea, and coffee, has had also a great hand in it. And the experience of making but slight suppers, or rather of turning suppers into beverages, has proved so conducive to health, that few people in England make a set supper. Whereas, beyond sea, 'tis counted the principal meal. . . .

The use of coffee and tea, two sober liquors now so prevalent in England, does take off people considerably from drinking of strong liquors. And, were it but for that, the coffee-houses ought to be kept up and encouraged.

Now coffee is made with the berries of a tree that grows in the Levant, and tea with the leaves of an India plant; both hot and dry, and therefore very proper for phlegmatic people. And, whereas strong liquors are apt to disorder the brain, these on the contrary do settle and compose it. Which makes it so much used by men of learning and business, who know best the virtue of 'em.

As for tobacco, the use whereof is indeed more universal, 'tis a remedy for phlegmatic people, and consequently not amiss in this country. 'Tis a companion in solitude, an amusement in company, an innocent diversion to melancholy, and a help to fancy in private studies and meditations. . . .

Besides the conveniency of traveling by water, either by sea, or here and there upon rivers, I may say the English nation is the best provided of any for land-travel, as to horses and coaches. And the truth is, there is not perhaps a country so proper for it, 'tis generally so open and level.

Traveling on horseback is so common a thing in England, that the meanest sort of people use it as well as the rest. Which sometimes fills the roads with riders, not without frequent disputes about giving the way, which is unusual beyond sea. And, as English horses are the best for expedition, so 'tis rare upon the road to see an Englishman but upon the gallop.

But for persons that are tender, or disabled, England excels all other nations in conveniency of coaches, but especially in that of stage-coaches; a very commodious and easy way of traveling. Here one may be transported without over-violent motion, and sheltered from the injuries of the air, to most noted places in England. With so much speed, that some of these coaches will reach above 50 miles in a summer day; and at so easy rates, that it is in some places less than a shilling for every five miles. . . .

To conclude now with the great trade of England to foreign parts, besides the several companies I have took notice of in my description of London, there are other companies or societies of merchants, established for the promoting or encouraging of foreign trade. Which have power and immunities granted them to make acts and orders, for the benefit of commerce in general, and other their companies in particular. Such are amongst other, the Company of Merchant Adventurers, the Russia, Turkey, and East-India Companies, and the Royal African Company. Besides the Spanish, French, East Land, and Greenland Companies, and the Company trading to Hudson's Bay, the privileges and trade of which last were lately confirmed by Act of Parliament. . . .

But the greatest and most eminent company is that which manages the East-India trade, which begun likewise in Queen Elizabeth's time, anno. 1660. For the managing whereof, they employ a joint stock, and have a great house in Leanden-Hall-Street, called the East-India House. By which trade and stock they have built a great number of war-like ships, and brought hither those Indian commodities which before were brought to us by the Portuguese, being the first discoverers of the East-India passage.

So that by the East-India and the Levant Companies, England, and many other countries by their second transportation, have ever since been supplied with those rich merchandizes which Italy, Turkey, Arabia, Persia, India, and China yield; where they have their respective agents. On the coast of Coromandel is the Fort St. George, belonging to the East-India Company, where they have a president of all the factories on that coast, and the Bay of Bengal.

As to the Royal African Company, King Charles II was pleased by his Letters Patent, to grant them a liberty of trading all along the western coasts of Africa, from Cape Vert as far as the Cape of Good Hope, with prohibition of trading there to all his other subjects. At Cape-Coast is the Residence of the chief Agent of the Company, where they have a strong place or fort. . . .

The principal commodities exported from hence into foreign countries are woolen cloths of all sorts, broad and narrow, the English being now the best cloth-workers in the world. To which add satins, tabbies, velvets, plushes, and infinite other manufactures; some of which make very good returns from the foreign plantations.

Abundance of tin, lead, alum, copper, iron, fuller earth, salt, and sea-coal, of most sorts of grains, but wheat especially, of skins and leather, of trane oil and tallow, hops and beer, saffron and licorice, besides great plenty of seafish, is yearly transported over sea to foreign countries.

From whence the merchants make good returns, and bring a great deal of treasure and rich commodities, to the enriching of themselves, the unspeakable benefit of the nation, and the credit of the English in general. Who are as industrious and active, as fair dealers, and great undertakers as any nation in the world.

10

The Effects of the New Long-Distance Trades

1695

This anonymous pamphlet on trade enunciates a common theme from late-seventeenth-century discussions. Long-distance commerce had vitally changed the nature of the European state. Classical and Renaissance texts about politics had to be reevaluated in light of modern realities. Since war was the most expensive activity of early modern states, the ability to raise money in new ways fundamentally changed what states could do. The issues highlighted in this pamphlet were commonplace. Similar claims were advanced in treatises written all over Europe in the late seventeenth and early eighteenth centuries.

Considerations Requiring Greater Care for Trade in England, and Some Expedients Proposed (London: printed for S. Crouch, 1695), 1–3.

'Tis very well known, that since the discovery of the East and West
Indies, and increase of navigation thereon, the state of Europe in general, and every nation in it in particular, is much altered, more especially in the course of war; for whereas before it was supplied by
soldiers, either voluntary or bound thereto by tenure of lands, who
found their own arms and clothes, and for a certain time provisions; so
that war was but of little expense to the state, and often decided by a
field-battle (as that between Algiers and Tunis last year) whereupon
the men went every one home again to his own house; now we see all
corners of Europe crowded with listed, disciplined, and standing
armies in pay, which as it cannot be done without huge funds of
money, and the ancient demesnes[14] of princes not sufficing, taxes are
every where increased on the subject; to the end the fountains of
which may be kept open, as 'tis reciprocally needful the state should
by all means consult increase of wealth to the people, (no other ways
supplied so well as by home manufacture and foreign trade) accordingly a change of the management of war in Europe is not more obvious, than the methods used to furnish necessary deniers for it in the
subject: therefore in this age, not only republics, but even the most
absolute monarchies, do sedulously court improvement of their wealth
by trade, witness France and Sweden, Florence, nay, the Popedom;
nor are we so to dread the monster arbitrary power, as to conceive the
same considerations that lead every man to proportion burdens to
the strength of his animal, and yield a pasture to the milch kine,[15] will
not also cherish so much mercy and goodness in the worst princes, as
not to extort more from their subjects than they have any means or
ability to raise.

Nothing is more demonstrative than . . . no money, no soldiers; and
no greater obstruction to the success of arms than want of pay, besides the increasing use of fortifications, artillery, and fire-engines is
costly; wherefore that state which has most money, may have most
men, and will be most like to have her enterprises succeed: Whoever
thinks the valor of a few may counter-balance the numbers of an enemy, or that an inexperienced army can stand against a veteran, will
run mighty hazard of being deceived; and though the English ancient
victories in France were sufficient to breed in us a conclusion of the
former, yet now a change of the discipline of arms puts men under a
nearer equality, so that whoever considers the course of our late and

[14]Personal lands of the prince or king.
[15]Milk cow.

present wars, may observe the aggressor mostly to exceed in number; besides war now a days is not determined by point of honor, and dint of sword, so much as by manifold intrigues, wherein gold has obtained the reputation of a virtue superlative.

As an alteration of the state of war in Europe requires usual supplies of money from the subject, 'tis as certain the support of estates in peace does now also call for supplies much enhanced of those in former ages, for demesnes, the ancient support of crowns, are generally embezzled, the nature and form of courts, the course of alliances, intrigues, and negotiations are altered, officers of all sorts multiplied, frauds complicate and inveterate, besides the occurrence of standing troops. Wherefore I conclude some extraordinary care is to be taken, that increase of wealth in the subjects may enable them to bear such new burdens; for if maintenance of the state require increase of revenue when the subject's purse is exhausted, as in the present case of Denmark, it must needs make both king and people uneasy; and whatever country this happen in will be exposed to danger of becoming a prey to some other.

11

The Rise of the Coffeehouse

1673

England's first coffeehouse opened in Oxford in 1650. Soon coffeehouses were opening all over the country. London had several hundred, perhaps over one thousand, by 1700. But coffeehouses were not merely metropolitan phenomena. By the 1670s, most English, Scottish, and Irish towns of any size had their own coffeehouse. The new coffeehouses had a culture wholly distinct from the older taverns and alehouses. They tended to be socially diverse, light and open, and controversial. This was mostly because they became known as places to gather news and information. Newspapers, manuscript newsletters, pamphlets, and gossip were freely dispensed in the coffeehouses. Charles II and James II both tried and

---

Coffee-houses Vindicated (London, 1673), 3–5.

failed to suppress the new institution. The anonymous pamphlet reproduced here was typical of many such publications debating the virtues and vices of the new institution. Although we tend to think of England as a tea-drinking country, it was instrumental in bringing the institution of the coffeehouse from the Middle East to Western Europe. Coffeehouses opened in Paris, Vienna, and Berlin decades after the first coffeehouse opened its doors in England. Those continental coffeehouses tended to be more expensive and hence more socially exclusive.

The dull planet Saturn has not finished one revolution through his orb since coffeehouses were first known amongst us, yet it is worth our wonder to observe how numerous they are already grown, not only here in our metropolis, but in both universities and most cities and eminent towns throughout the nation; Nor indeed have we any places of entertainment of more use and general convenience in several respects amongst us. . . .

In regard of easy expense, being to wait for or meet a friend, a tavern reckoning soon breeds a purse consumption. In an ale house you must gorge yourself with pot after pot, sit dully alone or be drawn into club for other reckoning, be frowned on by your landlady as one that cumbers the house and hinders better guests, but here for a penny or two you may spend two or three hours, have the shelter of a house, the warmth of a fire, the diversion of company and conveniency if you please of taking a pipe of tobacco. And all this without any grumbling or repining. . . .

For diversion, it is older than Aristotle, and will be true when Hobbes[16] is forgotten, that man is a sociable creature and delights in company. Now where shall a person wearied with hard study or the laborious turmoils of a tedious day repair to refresh himself, or where can young gentlemen or shopkeepers more innocently and advantageously spend an hour or two in the evening than at a coffeehouse, where they shall be sure to meet company, and by the custom of the house not such as at other places stingy and reserved to themselves, but free and communicative, where every man may modestly begin his story, and propose to, or answer another as he thinks fit; . . . The mind's best diet and the great whetstone and incentive of ingenuity, by

[16]Thomas Hobbes (1588–1679), English philosopher.

that we come to know men better than by their physiognomies, . . . *Speak that I may see you* was the philosopher's adage, to read men is acknowledged more useful than books, but where is there a better library for that study generally than here, amongst such a variety of humors all expressing themselves on diverse subjects according to their respective abilities? . . .

Besides, how infinitely are the vain pratings of these ridiculous pragmatics over-balanced by the sage and solid reasoning here frequently to be heard of experienced gentlemen, judicious lawyers, able physicians, ingenious merchants, and understanding citizens, in the abstrusest points of reason, philosophy, law and public commerce?

In brief it is undeniable that as you have here the most civil so it is generally the most intelligent society, the frequenting whose converse, and observing their discourses and department cannot but civilize our manners, enlarge our understandings, refine our language, teach us a generous confidence and handsome mode of address, and brush off . . . (as I remember Tully[17] somewhere calls it) that clownish kind of modesty, frequently incident to the best natures, which renders them sheepish and ridiculous in company.

[17]Marcus Tullius Cicero, Roman philosopher.

Revolution in Politics

The Revolution of 1688–89 has usually been treated as a political revolution, a revolution that changed exclusively the constitutional arrangements of the English state. This section introduces the key constitutional document produced after the revolution and two opposing views of the proper nature of political power in England.

12

The Declaration of Rights
February 19, 1689

This joint declaration by the House of Lords and the House of Commons outlined the extralegal actions taken by James II and prohibited future kings and queens from repeating them. It is worth comparing this document to William's Declaration *(see Document 2). The document reprinted here was a declaration in that it did not claim to be making new law, but declaring old law. The key issue, as Colley Cibber notes in Document 5, was how to ensure that kings would follow constraints on their actions.*

The Declaration of the Lords Spiritual and Temporal, and Commons, assembled at Westminster.

Whereas the late King James the Second, by the assistance of diverse evil councilors, judges, and ministers, employed by him, did endeavor to subvert and extirpate the Protestant religion, and the laws and liberties of this kingdom....

... [T]he said Lords Spiritual and Temporal, and Commons, pursuant to their respective letters and elections, being now assembled in a full and free representative of this nation, taking into their most serious consideration the best means for attaining the ends aforesaid do, in the first place (as their ancestors, in like case, have usually done), for the vindication and asserting their ancient rights and liberties, declare:

That the pretended power of suspending of laws by regal authority without consent of Parliament is illegal;

That the pretended power of dispensing with laws, or the execution of laws, by regal authority, as it has been assumed and exercised of late, is illegal;

That the Commission for erecting the late Court of Commissioners for Ecclesiastical Causes, and all other commissions and courts of like nature, are illegal and pernicious;

That levying of money for or to the use of the crown by pretense of prerogative, without grant of Parliament, for longer time, or in other manner than the same is or shall be granted, is illegal;

That it is the right of the subjects to petition the King, and all commitments and prosecutions for such petitioning, are illegal;

That the raising or keeping a standing army within the kingdom in time of peace, unless it be with consent of Parliament, is against law;

That the subjects which are Protestants may have arms for their defense, suitable to their conditions, as allowed by law;

That election of members of Parliament ought to be free;

That the freedom and debates or proceeding in Parliament ought not to be impeached or questioned in any court or place out of Parliament;

That excessive bail ought not to be required, nor excessive fines imposed, nor cruel and unusual punishment inflicted;

That jurors ought to be impaneled and returned; and jurors, which pass upon men in trials for high treason, ought to be freeholders;

That all grants and promises of fines and forfeitures of particular persons, before conviction, are illegal and void;

And that, for redress of all grievances, and for the amending, strengthening, and preserving of the laws, Parliaments ought to be held frequently.

And they do claim, demand and insist upon, all and singular the premises, as their undoubted rights and liberties; and that no declarations, judgments, doings, or proceedings to the prejudice of the people, in any of the said premises, ought in anywise to be drawn hereafter into consequence, or example:

To which demand of their rights they are particularly encouraged by the Declaration of his Highness the Prince of Orange as being the only means for obtaining a full redress and remedy therein.

Having therefore an entire confidence that his said Highness the Prince of Orange will perfect the deliverance so far advanced by him, and will still preserve them from the violation of their rights, which they have here asserted, and from all other attempts upon their religion, rights, and liberties:

The said Lords Spiritual and Temporal, and Commons, assembled at Westminster, do resolve,

That William and Mary, Prince and Princess of Orange, be, and be declared, King and Queen of England, France, and Ireland, and the dominions thereunto belonging; to hold the crown and royal dignity of the said kingdoms and dominions to them, the said Prince and Princess, during their lives, and the life of the survivor of them; and that the sole and full exercise of the regal power be only in, and executed by, the said Prince of Orange, in the names of the said Prince and Princess during their joint lives; and, after their deceases, the said crown and royal dignity of the said kingdoms and dominions to be to the heirs of the body of the said Princess, and for default of such issue, to the Princess Anne of Denmark, and the heirs of her body, and, for default of such issue, to the heirs of the body of the said Prince of Orange.

And the said Lords Spiritual and Temporal, and Commons do pray the said Prince and Princess of Orange to accept the same accordingly. . . .

13

THOMAS CARTWRIGHT

A Defense of James II's View of the Constitution
February 1686

Thomas Cartwright (1634–1689) was one of the most prominent and vocal defenders of the rights of the crown during the reign of James II. He was preferred (promoted) to the Episcopal see of Chester in December 1686 and served loyally on James II's Ecclesiastical Commission. While this sermon was preached on the occasion of the anniversary of James II's accession, Cartwright was responding in part to the principles that he felt had spawned the Duke of Monmouth's rebellion the previous summer. Cartwright was loyal to James in the crisis of 1688–89, following his king to France in December 1688 and then to Ireland in the spring of 1689.

Our religion will never suffer us to dispense with our loyalty, to serve any worldly interest or advantage; no, not for its own defense. It sets the crown fast and easy upon the King's head, without catechizing

Thomas Cartwright, *A Sermon Preached upon the Anniversary Solemnity of the Inauguration of Our Dread Sovereign Lord King James II* (London, 1686), 13–39.

him: for be his heart inclinable to any religion, or none, it leaves him no rival, none to insult or lord it over him. It disclaims all usurpation, popular, or papal; neither pope nor presbyter may control him; none but the great God, the only ruler of princes, can over-rule him; to whom 'tis his duty, glory and happiness to be subject. Though the King should not please or humor us; though he should rend off the mantle from our bodies (as Saul did from Samuel[18]) nay though he should sentence us to death (of which, blessed be God and the King, there is no danger), yet, if we are living members of the Church of England, we must neither open our mouths, nor lift our hands against him; but honor him before the people and elders of Israel. . . .

Who questioned Saul for slaying the priests,[19] and revolting to idolatry? Who questioned Joram, a parricide and murderer of his nobles?[20] Or Joash, for his idolatry, and slaying the High-Priest?[21] Did the Sanhedrim do it? Who questioned Theodosius for murdering six thousand innocent persons?[22] Who questioned Constans, Valens, or Julian the apostate?[23] Who traduced their persons, or dignities, or offered them any tumultuous affronts, or remonstrances? So that unless we in these latter days, do understand the mind of God, better than the Jewish Church, and the primitive Christians did; we must not ask our Prince, why he governs us otherwise than we please to be governed ourselves. We must neither call him to account for his religion, nor question him for his policy in civil matters; for he is made our King by God's law, of which the law of the land is only declarative: 'tis God alone who can take vengeance of him, if he does amiss; and proportion punishments to his person. Upon his providence are we obliged to depend, who never fails to help religious men and kingdoms in their distresses, and makes all things work together for their good. . . .

. . . Did not God ordain Adam to rule over his wife, without giving her, or her children, any commission to limit his power? What was given to him in his person, was also given to his posterity; and the

---

[18] 1 Samuel 15:27–28.

[19] 1 Samuel 22.

[20] 2 Chronicles 21:4.

[21] 2 Chronicles 24:15–25.

[22] Theodosius I (r. 379–395 CE), Roman emperor. In 390, he ordered a retributive massacre in Thessalonica that claimed over six thousand lives in order to avenge the death of one of his generals in a riot.

[23] Roman emperors: Constans (r. 337–350 CE); Valens (r. 364–378 CE); and Julian (r. 361–363 CE), who was called "the Apostate" for his vigorous promotion of paganism and his disestablishment of the Christian church in the empire.

paternal government, continued monarchial from him to the flood; and after that to the confusion of Babel, when kingdoms were first erected and planted over the face of the earth: And so what right or title of the people can have, or what commission, either of limitation or mixture, to refrain that supremacy which was as unlimited in Adam as any act of will (it being due to the supreme fatherhood), or from what time it commenced, the scripture nowhere tells us. Where is the people's charter extant, either in nature or scripture, for invading the rights of the crown? Or what authority can they have from either to introduce their devices of presiding over him whom God and nature hath set over them? Nay, how vain and void of sense are all these popular projects? Who can set such bounds to his prerogative, as to impose penalties on him if he exceed, or put those conditional limitations in execution? Nor can the King himself divest of his supremacy, or discharge his subjects of their allegiance. And if any monarch will be so freehearted, as to lay down his lawful power at his subjects feet; if he will throw up that commission which he had from God, independent of any other, and take a new one from his subjects (as some inferior magistrates do from him) ... during the pleasure of our sovereign lords the people; he forgets that it was a divine hand coming out of the clouds which set the crown on his head; and that when there was but one good king upon the face of the earth (only Solomon), their original was derived from God above, and not from the people beneath. For 'twas God himself who best knew it, that said, "By me Kings reign."

Be their religion and administration of their office what pleases them, they are of God's making, and must not be of the people's marring.

Our King comes to his crown by lineal descent, from the loins of our David. He is no alien or stranger to the royal race, nor does his promotion come either from the East, or from the West. But 'tis God who hath set him over us, with his holy oil hath he anointed him and set him on his father's throne. 'Tis to God's grace alone, that we owe our King; and by the royal concessions of him, and his ancestors, do we enjoy our liberties and prosperities: and the duty of subjects to their princes, of servants to their masters, and of children to their parents, is obliging to them, though they never swore to do it; or 'tis not the result of Christianity or policy, but a principle of nature, which religion doth not alter, but establish. Though Darius were an alien, and an enemy to his religion, compelling to idolatry, and kept the people of God in captivity as slaves; yet Daniel paid him the homage of a good

subject, after he had been shut up in the lion's den.[24] He acknowledged him to be his king, and honored him accordingly; O King live
forever: And the primitive Christians wished Julian himself, length of
days and prosperity.[25] . . .

Alas! We do but flatter ourselves, if ever we hope to be governed,
without that which is commonly called an arbitrary power (let the
word found never so harshly). The only question is, who shall have it?
Whether it shall be in the King, or the people? In one or many? And
the denial of necessary powers for the safety of the Kingdom, which
(call them what you will) are the regalia, the inherent rights of the
crown, for fear of misgovernment, is the ready way to lose all the
fruits and benefits of government itself, for want of those powers to
support it. For 'tis impossible for any commonwealth to subsist, without the dreadful thing, called arbitrary power (if by arbitrary you
mean, as I do, supreme and absolute). True it is, that if this be vested
in one, the people are over-apt to call it tyranny; but if many, they
are pleased to christen it, by the glorious name of liberty: though if
tyranny consist not in the abundance, but abuse of power; not in the
uncontrollableness, but unreasonableness; not in the exercise, but
excess of it; it will be as unjust and tyrannical in them, as in him, so
to use it. Nor are commonwealths more secured from this sort of
tyranny than monarchies. Our own statute laws acknowledge, that our
King is subject to none but God; and that he has an imperial crown;
and they call his Kingdom an empire: and by the common law, the
King is neither inferior to the three estates, nor co-ordinate with
them . . . greater than all of them, as well collectively, as singly. The
parliament doth but propound, prepare, and present the project of law;
'tis the royal stamp that makes it one: The sole legislative power is
lodged in the King; and to him (says Bracton[26]) belongs the interpretation of all laws, when made (not in plain cases, but in new questions,
and emergent doubts) of which the King was the first, and must be
the last judge too: For if the people be judge, he is no monarch at all;
and so farewell all government.

---

[24]Though unknown to history, Darius the Mede was, according to the Book of
Daniel, the first Persian king of Babylon (Daniel 5:31).
[25]That is, despite the Emperor Julian's apostasy from Christianity.
[26]Sir Henry Bracton (c. 1210–1268), English jurist.

14

GILBERT BURNET

A Defense of the Williamite View of the Constitution

1688

Gilbert Burnet (1643–1715) was a Scottish Episcopalian who made a name for himself as a preacher and historian in London in the 1670s. He was closely associated with Whig political circles and low church religious groups. He fled England before James came to the throne, and after traveling through Europe, he settled in the Netherlands. There he became closely associated with William III. The pamphlet excerpted here, written by Burnet, was illegally and widely circulated in England before William's arrival in November 1688. After the revolution, Burnet was rewarded with the see of Salisbury. He remained a prominent religious and political figure until his death in 1715.

That as the light of nature has planted in all men a natural principle of the love of life, and of a desire to preserve it; so the common principles of all religions agree in this, that God having set us in this world, we are bound to preserve that being, which he has given us, by all just and lawful ways. Now this duty of self-preservation is exerted in instances of two sorts. The one are, in the resisting of violent aggressors; the other are the taking of just revenges of those, who have invaded us so secretly, that we could not prevent them, and so violently that we could not resist them: in which cases the principle of self-preservation warrants us, both to recover what is our own, with just damages, and also to put such unjust persons out of a capacity of doing the like Injuries any more, either to ourselves, or to any others. Now in these instances of self-preservation, this difference is to be observed; that the first cannot be limited, by any slow forms, since a pressing danger requires a vigorous repulse; and cannot admit of delays; whereas the second, of taking revenges, or reparations, is not of such haste, but that it may be brought under rules and forms. . . .

Gilbert Burnet, *An Enquiry into the Measures of Submission to the Supream Authority* (London, 1688), 1–8.

3. The true and original notion of a civil society and government is, that it is a compromise made by such a body of men, by which they resign up the right of demanding reparations, either in the way of justice, against one another, or in the way of war, against their neighbors; to such a single person or to such a body of men as they think fit to trust with this. And in the management of this civil society, great distinction is to be made between the power of making laws for the regulating the conduct of it, and the power of executing those laws: the supreme authority must still be supposed to be lodged with those who have the legislative power reserved to them; but not with those who have only the executive; which is plainly a trust, when it is separated from the legislative power; and all trusts, by their nature import that those to whom they are given are accountable, even though that it should not be expressly specified in the words of the trust itself.

4. It cannot be supposed by the principles of natural religion, that God has authorized any one form of government, any other way than as the general rules of order and of justice oblige ᵃll men not to subvert constitutions, nor disturb the peace of mankiᵈ ᵈ, or invade those rights with which the law may have vested some persons. For it is certain, that as private contracts lodge or translate private rights, so the public laws can likewise lodge such rights, prerogatives and revenues, in those under whose protection they put themselves, and in such a manner that they may come to have as good a title to these as any private person can have to his property: so that it becomes an act of high injustice and violence, to invade these: which is so far a greater sin than any such actions would be against a private person, as the public peace and order is preferable to all private considerations whatsoever. So that in truth, the principles of natural religion give those that are in authority no power at all, but they do only secure them in the possession of that which is theirs by law. . . .

6. It is certain, that God, as the creator and governor of the world, may set up whom he will to rule over other men. But this declaration of his will must be made evident by prophets or other extraordinary men sent of him, which have some manifest proofs of the divine authority that is committed to them, on such occasions, and upon such persons declaring the will of God, in favor of any others, that declaration is to be submitted to, and obeyed. But this pretence of a divine delegation can be carried no further than to those who are thus expressly marked out, and is unjustly claimed by those who can prove no such declaration to have been ever made in favor of them or their families. Nor does it appear reasonable to conclude from their being in

possession, that it is the will of God that it should be so. This justifies all usurpers, when they are successful.

7. The measures of power and, by consequence, of obedience must be taken from the express laws of any state, or body of men, from the oaths that they swear, or from immemorial prescription, and a long possession, which both give a title, and in a long tract of time make a bad one become good, since prescription when it passes the memory of man, and is not disputed by any other pretender, gives by the common sense of all men a just and good title: so upon the whole matter, the degrees of all civil authority, are to be taken either from express laws, immemorial customs, or from particular oaths which the subjects swear to their princes: this being still laid down for a principle that in all the disputes between power and liberty proves itself; the one being founded only upon positive law, and the other upon the law of nature. . . .

11. We are then at last brought to the constitution of our English government: so that no general considerations from speculations about sovereign power, nor from any passages either of the Old and New Testament, ought to determine us in this matter, which must be fixed from the laws and regulations that have been made among us. It is then certain, that with relation to the executive part of the government, the law has lodged that singly in the King; so that the whole administration of it is in him: but the legislative power is lodged between the King and the two houses of Parliament; so that the power of making and repealing laws is not singly in the King, but only so far as the two houses concur with him. It is also clear that the King has such a determined extent of prerogative beyond which he has no authority: as for instance, if he levies money of his people, without a law empowering him to do it, he goes beyond the limits of his power, and asks that to which he has no right: so that there lies no obligation on the subject to grant it: and if any in his name use violence for the obtaining it, they are to be looked on as so many robbers that invade our property, and they being violent aggressors, the principle of preservation seems here to take place and to warrant as violent a resistance.

12. There is nothing more evident than that England is a free nation that has its liberties and properties reserved to it by many positive and express laws: if then we have a right to our property, we must likewise be supposed to have a right to preserve it: for those rights are by the law secured against the invasions of the prerogative, and by consequence we must have a right to preserve them against

those invasions. It is also evidently declared by our law that all orders and warrants that are issued out in opposition to them are null of themselves; and by consequence, any that pretend to have commissions from the King for those ends are to be considered as if they had none at all: since those commissions being void of themselves, are indeed no commissions in the construction of the law; and therefore those who act in virtue of them are still to be considered as private persons who come to invade and disturb us. It is also to be observed that there are some points that are justly disputable and doubtful, and others that are so manifest that it is plain that any objections that can be made to them are rather forced pretences than so much as plausible colors. It is true, if the case is doubtful, the interest of the public peace and order ought to carry it; but the case is quite different when the invasions that are made upon liberty and property are plain and visible to all that consider them. . . .

14. Here is the true difficulty of this whole matter, and therefore it ought to be exactly considered: First, all general words, how large soever, are still supposed to have a tacit exception and reserve in them, if the matter seems to require it. Children are commanded to obey their parents in all things; wives are declared by the scripture, to be subject to their husbands in all things, as the church is unto Christ: and yet how comprehensive soever these words may seem to be, there is still a reserve to be understood in them; and though by our form of marriage, the parties swear to one another 'till death them do part, yet few doubt but that this bond is dissolved by adultery, though it is not named; for odious things ought not to be suspected, and therefore not named upon such occasions. But when they fall out, they carry still their own force with them. 2. When there seems to be a contradiction between two articles in the constitution, we ought to examine which of the two is most evident, and the most important, and so we ought to fix upon it, and then we must give such an accommodating sense to that which seems to contradict it, that so we may reconcile those together. Here then are two seeming contradictions in our constitution: The one is the public liberty of the nation; the other is the renouncing of all resistance, in case that we're invaded. It is plain that our liberty is only a thing that we enjoy at the King's discretion and during his pleasure, if the other against all resistance is to be understood according to the utmost extent of the words. Therefore since the chief design of our whole law, and of all the several rules of our constitution, is to secure and maintain our liberty, we ought to lay that down for a conclusion, that it is both the most plain and the most

important of the two: And therefore the other article against resistance ought to be so softened, as that it does not destroy this. 3. Since it is by a law that resistance is condemned, we ought to understand it in such a sense as that it does not destroy all other laws; And therefore the intent of this law must only relate to the executive power, which is in the King, and not to the legislative, in which we cannot suppose that our legislators, who made that law, intended to give up that which we plainly see they resolved still to preserve entire, according to the constitution. So then, the not resisting the King can only be applied to the executive power, that so upon no pretence of ill administrations in the execution of the law, it should be lawful to resist him; but this cannot with any reason be extended to an invasion of the legislative power, or to a total subversion of the government. For it being plain that the law did not design to lodge that power in the King, it is also plain that it did not indeed to secure him in it, in case he should set about it. 4. The law mentioning the King, or those commissioned by him, shows plainly; that it [is] only designed to secure the King in the executive power: for the word commission necessarily imports this, since if it is not according to law, it is no commission; and by consequence, those who act in virtue of it, are not commissioned by the King in the sense of the law. The King likewise imports a prince clothed by law with the regal prerogative; but if he goes to subvert the whole foundation of the government, he subverts that by which he himself has his power, and by consequence he annuls his own power; and then he ceases to be King, having endeavored to destroy that upon which his own authority is founded. . . .

The next thing to be considered, is to see in fact whether the foundations of this government have been struck at, and whether those errors that have been perhaps permitted, are only such mal-versions, as ought to be imputed only to human frailty, and to the ignorance, inadvertencies, or passions to which all princes may be subject, as well as other men. But this will best appear if we consider what are the fundamental points of our government, and the chief securities that we have for our liberties.

The authority of the law is indeed all in one word, so that if the King pretends to a power to dispense with laws, there is nothing left upon which the subject can depend; and yet as if dispensing power were not enough, if laws are wholly suspended for all time coming, this is plainly a repealing of them, when likewise the men, in whose hands the administration of justice is put by law, such as judges and sheriffs, are allowed to tread all laws under foot, even those that infer an incapacity on themselves if they violate them; this is such a breaking of the whole constitution, that we can no more have the administration of justice, so that it is really a dissolution of the government; since all trials, sentences, and the executions of them, are become so many unlawful acts, that are null and void of themselves.

The next thing in our Constitution, which secures to us our laws and liberties, is a free and lawful Parliament. Now not to mention the breach of the law of triennial Parliaments, it being above three years since we had a session that enacted any law; methods have been taken, and are daily taken, that render this impossible. Parliaments ought to be chosen with an entire liberty, and without either force of pre-engagements: whereas if all men are required beforehand to enter into engagements, how they will vote if they are chosen themselves, or how they will give their voices in the electing of others? This is plainly such a preparation to a Parliament, as would indeed make it no Parliament, but a cabal, if one were chosen, after all that corruption of persons who had pre-engaged themselves; and after the threatening and turning out of all persons of employments who had refused to do it; and if there are such daily regulations made in the towns, that it is plain those who manage them intend at last to put such a number of men in the corporations as will certainly choose the persons who are recommended to them. But above all, if there are such a number of sheriffs and mayors made, over England, by whom the elections must be conducted and returned, who are now under an incapacity by law, and so are no legal officers, and by consequence those elections that pass under their authority are null and void. If, I say, it is clear that things are brought to this, than the government is dissolved, because it is impossible to have a free and legal Parliament in this state of things. If then both the authority of the law and the constitution of the Parliament are struck at and dissolved, here is a plain subversion of the whole government. But if we enter next into the particular branches of the government, we will find the like disorder among them all.

The Protestant Religion, and the Church of England, make a great article of our government, the latter being secured not only of old by Magna Charta, but by many special laws made of late; and there are particular laws made in K. Charles the First, the late King's time [Charles II], securing them from all commissions that the King can raise for judging or censuring them: if then in opposition to this, a court so condemned is erected, which proceeds to judge and censure the clergy, and even to dis-seize them of their freeholds, without so much as the form of a trial, though this is the most indispensable law of all those that secures the property of England; and if the King pretends that he can require the clergy to publish all his arbitrary declarations, and in particular one that strikes at their whole settlement, and has ordered process to be begun against all that disobeyed this illegal warrant and has treated so great a number of the bishops as criminals, only for representing to him the reasons of their not obeying him; if likewise the King is not satisfied to profess his own religion openly, though even that is contrary to law, but has sent ambassadors to Rome, and received nuncios from thence, which is plainly treason by law; if likewise many popish churches and chapels have been publicly opened; if several colleges of Jesuits have been set up in diverse parts of the nation, and one of the order has been made a Privy Councilor and a principal minister of state; and if Papists, and even those who turn to that religion, though declared traitors by law, are brought into all the chief employments, both military and civil; than it is plain, that all the rights of the Church of England, and the whole establishment of the Protestant religion are struck at, and designed to be overturned; since all these things, as they are notoriously illegal, so they evidently demonstrate, that the great design of them all, is the rooting out of this pestilent heresy, in their style, I mean the Protestant religion.

In the next place, if in the whole course of justice, it is visible, that there is a constant practicing upon the judges, that they are turned out upon their varying from the intentions of the court, and if men of no reputation nor abilities are put in their places; if an army is kept up in time of peace, and men who withdraw from that illegal service are hanged up as criminals, without any color of law, which by consequence are so many murders; and of the soldiery are connived at and encouraged in the most enormous crimes, that so they may be thereby prepared to commit greater ones, and from single rapes and murders proceed to rape upon all our liberties and a destruction of the nation: if, I say, all these things are true in fact, then it is plain, that there is such a dissolution of government made, that there is not any one part of it left found and entire: and if all these things are done now, it is easy to imagine what may be expected, when arbitrary power that spares no man, and popery that spares no heretic, are finally established. Then we may look for nothing but gabelles, tailles,[27] impositions, benevolences, and all sorts of illegal taxes, as from the other we may expect burnings, massacres, and inquisitions. . . .

---

[27]Two of the more unpopular French taxes. The *gabelle* was a tax on salt; the *taille* was a direct tax on personal possessions.

If all these matters are true in fact, then I suppose no man will doubt, that the whole foundations of this government, and all the most sacred parts of it, are overturned; and as to the truth of all the suppositions, that is left to every Englishman's judgment and sense.

Revolution in Foreign Policy

European developments have always played a role in interpretations of the Revolution of 1688–89. However, scholars have traditionally consigned the European context to assessments of William's motives. William, most historians agree, descended on England in the autumn of 1688 in part to provoke a realignment that would serve to contain the growing power of Louis XIV of France. Continental developments, it is said, held little interest for James II, who expended his energies primarily on domestic affairs. And thus William, we are told, was forced to impose his anti-French foreign policy as a condition of accepting the crown. The documents in this section have been selected to test this traditional narrative. Was there a popular English discussion of foreign affairs before the revolution? Did James II have clear foreign policy priorities? And if so, how did these accommodate his domestic agenda? Was the postrevolutionary war against France simply a Williamite imposition, or had England undergone a transformation in international orientation?

15

Court Memorandum on Foreign Affairs
August 2, 1686

This anonymous court memorandum was copied by the Spanish ambassador to England, Don Pedro Ronquillo. The anti-Dutch arguments produced in this excerpt were nothing new. They were the same kinds of arguments adduced in favor of going to war against the Dutch in the 1660s and 1670s. In both cases, James had been one of the prime hawks.

British Library, Add. MSS 34502, f. 79r.

That the injuries and injustices committed by the Dutch against [James II] and his subjects are insupportable, and that there is no appearance of receiving any reparation. That they have fomented the last rebellion[28] and give every asylum to His Majesty's rebels, and that we shall never see the last of their factions until that republic is destroyed . . . there never was such an opportunity to destroy them as the present, when all the forces that would assist them are employed against the Turks, and that they are assured on good authority the Turks will not so soon make peace. That if this opportunity is allowed to pass by, [James II's] own subjects as well as the Dutch will become insolent, and he will be despised by the whole earth; that the factions and principally those of Orange, will increase so much that they will continue to change his resolutions with regard to religion and his prerogative, and give to the Prince of Orange as successor, almost the whole government.

[28]A reference to the widespread belief that the Dutch had actively supported the rebellions of the Duke of Monmouth.

16

Catholic Court Memorandum

November 9, 1686

This anonymous memorandum of unknown provenance was clearly produced by a Roman Catholic insider at James II's court. Unlike Document 15, which rehashed time-tested anti-Dutch arguments, this memo raised concerns specific to James II's regime.

I cannot choose therefore but think, that nothing can be of greater danger to his Majesty's safety or repose whilst he lives; nor a more certain ruin, destruction and extirpation of the Catholics in this kingdom after his decease than a continuance of that coldness [there] seems at present to be betwixt his Majesty and the princess of Orange, whose husband by his martial virtues and presbyterian education seems to

Beinecke Rare Book and Manuscript Library, Yale University, Osborne MSS 2/Box 4/Folder 76.

me a very dangerous center for the wishes and hopes of all the discontented and disloyal part of the three kingdoms, and should any disobligations so far provoke him to forget his duty as to become their head, nothing could be more fatal: for I fear his Majesty would in such case find but very cold assistance from his lukewarm army: a more seditious and malignant spirit reigning in no part of his dominions more than in that, whatever some politicians about him do make him believe to the contrary.

If all this I have said be true, and that the Prince however should never defect from his duty so far as to give his Majesty any willful disturbance in his lifetime, yet a bare coldness between them, will continue a vigorous hope in the faction, and render all his Majesty's endeavors for a Catholic and national interest feeble and ineffectual to his perpetual disturbance and the diminution of his glory, nor will the divided interest of the royal family fail to be imputed to popish councils and endeavors, and will as surely be revenged upon them accordingly in the next successor's reign, should God deny his Majesty a son to succeed him.

For if we reflect that the number of Catholics is not only inconsiderable to the nation and that none to speak of amongst them neither are employed in trade or business but depend on lands and are generally those the Dutch call idlemen, a general extirpation of them by banishment will be reckoned no greater a loss to the kingdom than if some sickly year had swept away twenty thousand people extraordinary. But their great estates will be a certain gain to the Prince and his courtiers that seizes them as well as the church lands were to the first reformers whose negative faith would have had but small success without those sensible arguments. And was there but half as much to be gained by bringing in religion as there was by suppressing of it, we should see more converts quickly.

17

ARNOUD VAN CITTERS

Reports of Growing Anti-Dutch Hysteria

January 24 and February 3, 1688

Arnoud Van Citters (1633–1696) was the Dutch ambassador to England during the reign of James II. In these diplomatic dispatches, he reported on the intense anti-Dutch sentiment at the court of James II.

24 January/3 February 1688

Those violent humors of wickedness, as it were, grind their teeth, and yet not wishing to desist from their designs, but seek to effect them *quovis modo,*[29] their advice might now lead that way to act again on their former projected plan [of 1686] which is to attack our republic, which they consider the only cause of all their obstacles, and as they think that as long as it stands all His Majesty's intentions cannot succeed. . . . I hear that in their Councils and daily discourses nothing else is now spoken of but *Delenda Carthago,*[30] which undoubtedly augment now daily.

3 February 1688

The evening before yesterday the King entered into conversation with the Pope's Nuncius . . . in which among other things he brought it *a propos,* how at his reiterated instances he had not been able to obtain so much from their High Mightinesses [the States General] as that of delivering up to him Dr. [Gilbert] Burnet, or to cause him to quit their provinces, and adding to this that this might serve as a good pretext,

---

[29] In whatever manner.

[30] "Carthage must be destroyed!": Cato's (234–149 BCE) refrain in the interim between the Second and Third Punic Wars. The fabled commercial prosperity of Carthage made its comparison to the Dutch Republic seem particularly apt. This cry was famously made in Parliament just prior to the Anglo-Dutch War of 1672–74.

British Library, Add. MSS 34512, ff. 69–70, 83–84.

as it clearly went contrary to the treaties [between England and the Dutch Republic] to declare war upon it . . . as if the inclinations existed for it.

18

ROGER MORRICE

War against the Dutch Republic as an Inevitability
February 4, 1688

Long before the Invitation of the Seven (see Document 1), Londoners believed that a war between England and the Netherlands was inevitable. Roger Morrice was a politically well-connected Nonconformist cleric. His "Ent'ring Book" (diary) provides us with one of the most detailed records of political gossip, religious sentiment, and social attitudes in late-seventeenth-century England.

There is nothing else universally discoursed on in London but that England and France will join in a war against the Dutch. And that we have ordered 25 sail of capital ships immediately to be set forth, which number will make up the ships we have abroad, and our Summer sea guard [is] 60 sail at least, and further that we are everyday carrying ammunition stores, guns, etc. to our ships.

Roger Morrice, "Ent'ring Book," February 4, 1688, Doctor Williams' Library, MSS 31Q, 236.

19

JAMES II

Thoughts on the Revolution

1690s

James II wrote lengthy manuscript memoirs when in exile in France.
He made the Scots College in Paris, a Catholic seminary, the official
archive for his reign. In the eighteenth century many came to read and
take notes from these memoirs. Unfortunately, the originals were de-
stroyed during the French Revolution. This selection, commenting on the
threat posed by William III throughout his reign, is based on an early-
nineteenth-century edition, based in turn on a transcript taken in the
eighteenth century.

At first sight indeed no one wondered that a people jealous of their
religion and liberty should be alarmed to see a Prince of a different
persuasion maintain a standing army in time of peace, but the argument seemed stronger when by those of the other party it was
returned upon themselves, for how much more reason, said they, had
he to apprehend danger from a people who had used his royal father
so ill because they only suspected him to be inclined to that religion of
which he had declared himself a member? He saw a factious party
both in the people and Parliament, laboring to possess the nation with
apprehensions not only of the popish religion, but popish violence too,
that two rebellious armies had already been brought into the field
upon that pretense, and he had great ground to expect a third would
not be long behind them. Whereas on the other hand, what probability
was there of his being able to establish popery with a Protestant army,
did he design it, or with a handful of his own people subjugate a
nation, which the power of Rome, when it governed the world, was
never able to make an absolute conquest of. Had the King (said they)
apprehended his factious subjects only, he might perhaps have ven-
tured himself upon the fidelity of his loyal ones, but he saw a more

---

Rev. J. S. Clarke, ed., *The Life of James the Second, King of England by Himself, Etc.* (London, 1816), vol. 2, 57–59, 171–73, 181–82.

dangerous cloud still hanging over his head than that he had lately dispersed, the Prince of Orange's conduct had raised a suspicion of an ancient date, the late King made no mystery of declaring that he looked upon him as one that waited only for a fit opportunity to usurp the crown. His Majesty saw how the troops had been poisoned that came from Holland, how he had underhandedly assisted the Duke of Monmouth, and yet no man seemed more delighted at his ruin, for Monsieur Bentinck,[31] whom that Prince had sent upon this occasion to the King with many professions of kindness and proffers of service, was in a grievous agony when he understood the King was resolved to see the Duke as soon as he was made a prisoner. And though after inquiry he found he had said nothing of what he apprehended in relation to his master, yet he was never at quiet till his head was struck off, and this was so manifest to all that had any insight into affairs that my Lord Dartmouth,[32] when he returned from the execution and had given the King an account of what had passed, told him that he had got rid of one enemy, but had still remaining a much more considerable and dangerous one behind, to wit the Prince of Orange. Those therefore who were favorable to the King's inclinations, and knew that the Prince of Orange was not an enemy to be slighted, saw plainly that nothing but an army could fence the King from that and other dangers, which not being contrary to any express law, nor as he managed it, any burden to the people, he merited (they said) rather the thanks, than the ill will, of his subjects for maintaining at his own expense, "a force so necessary not only for his own security but for the public tranquility at home, and the nation's credit abroad, which in a short time was become the envy of its neighbors, who began to be jealous of the flourishing condition His Majesty's just government had brought it to, in which they might have long continued had not the groundless apprehensions of the Church of England, blown up by the Prince of Orange's emissaries and the blackest calumnies of angry and implacable men, made the most zealous members of that Church quite forget their so much preached up doctrine of passive obedience to their lawful Prince," and justify His Majesty to the world, by a woeful example, how necessary it was for him to seek a more solid security than

---

[31] Hans Willem Bentinck, 1st Earl of Portland (1649?–1709), Dutch confidant, adviser, and emissary of William Prince of Orange both before and after the Revolution of 1688–89. He was made 1st Earl of Portland in April 1689.

[32] George Legge, 1st Baron Dartmouth (1648–1691), naval commander and veteran of both the Second and Third Anglo-Dutch Wars. An intimate of James II, he was named commander in chief of the navy in 1688.

the empty promises of the House of Commons, and those pompous expressions of loyalty, which he was not now to learn how little they were to be depended on in times of troubles and public discontent. . . .

And now the general discontent was grown to such a head that the Prince of Orange thought it ripe for his undertaking. He had long ambitioned the crown of England, and bore with great impatience the delay of a reversion, but now being cut off even from the expectancy by the birth of a Prince of Wales, was resolved to wait no longer, finding so favorable a disposition on all hands to second his attempt. First, from the factious temper of the people of England, and their inclination to change, and now especially, by reason of their disgust at the King's favoring Catholics and dispensing with certain laws which disposed them not only to receive the Prince of Orange, but invite him to their aid. However, all this would not have done his work had not the situation of affairs in other neighboring countries seconded his design: The House of Austria had for some time been projecting a formidable League against France, whose former acquisitions had given them great disquiet and made them apprehend new ones, so were resolved (if possible) to be beforehand with it now. The Prince of Orange's ambition to be at the head of a powerful army, and his inveterate enmity against that King, made him an earnest stickler in this League, which at last was concluded at Augsburg between the Empire, the kingdom of Spain, and the States of Holland, and they had found means to render the Pope himself (who was at that time ill-satisfied with the Court of France) to be more than favorable to their enterprise, so that nothing was wanting but the conjunction of England to make their force as formidable as they themselves could wish it. But a King (besides the little inclination he had to fall out with a Prince his near relation and ancient friend) having the prospect of enjoying a perfect peace and free trade, when all his neighbors should be engaged in war, made him give no ear to the earnest solicitations of the Emperor's and King of Spain's ambassadors, who pressed him violently to enter into this confederacy. They urged it upon him under the notion of being guaranteed of the Peace of Nijmegen,[33] but that was no reason, he said, why he should side with one party, and that too,

---

[33]The Peace of Nijmegen (1678–79) comprised a series of settlements between France, Spain, and the Dutch Republic and marked the conclusion of the Franco-Dutch War (1672–78). England had withdrawn from this conflict in 1674 with the signing of the Treaty of Westminster, which marked the end of the Third Anglo-Dutch War (1672–74).

which was resolved to be the aggressor. Besides, that obligation (if any) was personal and ended with his brother, but (as was already observed) His Majesty made appear, there was no such obligation upon him, for the Dutch having clapped up a separate peace without the privity of the King's Ministers, they had orders not to sign even as mediators, much less as guarantees. Besides, His Majesty looked upon the imagination of an universal monarchy (with which they strove to fright him as a thing aimed at by France) as a fantastical dream, both impolitic and impracticable, as appeared by Charles the Fifth,[34] and Philip the Second,[35] but that were it otherwise, the situation of England still secured it so well against a French, or any other encroachment, that neutrality was its true interest, which made His Majesty grasp at this occasion of eating out the Dutch, the kingdom's rivals in trade, rather than to eat out his own people's bowels, in the defense of that Commonwealth, which never failed to leave their allies in the lurch at the least faint appearance of advantage by it. . . .

However nothing raised the King more enemies than this spiteful and groundless report of a league with France, which had no other origin but this. Nor is it to be wondered that the King of France (seeing the design of drawing His Majesty into the alliance against him, which he had the more reason to apprehend because there was in reality no such league between them, and by consequence no obligation to the contrary) should endeavor by this flight of generosity in offering him succors and threatening the Dutch in his behalf to work him to his interest, it was no wonder each party should labor to get England on its side, it was sure to weigh down the balance wherever it was cast, but the King was too good a Christian to invade a Prince he had no quarrel with, and too much an Englishman to engage with France against his subjects' inclinations. His intentions were to engross the trade of the world while foreign States destroyed each other, but the want of wit as well as loyalty in his subjects would not suffer them to be so happy. Fears of slavery amongst the gentry, and popery amongst the clergy, were so artificially spread as bewitched the people, not only to their ruin, but to be themselves the instruments of it; so the King suffered for his goodwill to the people, and the people were punished sufficiently for their folly and rebellion. The Dutch indeed gained their point and drew in the English rather to

[34]Charles V (1500–1558), king of Spain (r. 1515–56) and Holy Roman Emperor (r. 1519–58).
[35]Philip II (1527–1598), king of Spain (r. 1556–98).

dethrone their King, than not to have their share in an expensive and bloody war, where nothing was to be got for themselves, instead of enjoying peace and a flourishing trade which their Prince designed them, and was thus rewarded by them for his good will.

20

Anti-Dutch Propaganda

1688

When it became clear that William intended to invade England based on his belief that there would be support in England for his cause, James II's propagandists quickly produced this pamphlet for popular consumption. This pamphlet, which was widely distributed in the autumn of 1688, reprised many of the themes from the court memoranda of 1686, as well as many of the old arguments against the Dutch from the earlier Anglo-Dutch Wars. The same kinds of arguments about Dutch materialism, high taxation, irreligion, and republicanism were repeated in government newsletters and in popular ballads. While the author of this work is unknown, its publication history makes it clear that it was produced on orders from James II's government.

The true motives and first springs of this design on the part of the States[36] must have been the care of preserving their trade, which is the only enriching of that country, and the means which has principally conduced to the establishing of that is the liberty of conscience they allow. Now, it is well known that in a great part of the world the subjects of our King and of the States share this advantage of traffic, and it is notoriously known by what perfidiousness, over-reaching and barbarity, the Dutch have wormed us out of the trade of the East-Indies, and that their unjust dealing has hitherto occasioned great wars betwixt England and the United Provinces.

[36]The United Provinces (Dutch Republic).

The Dutch Design Anatomized (London, 1688), 7–8, 15–17, 20–21.

They, therefore finding that our King's inclinations were such to establish liberty of conscience, foresaw the ill consequences of it to themselves because we, having more convenient ports, a richer soil, and a more numerous people, by this very liberty should draw many industrious persons hither who might live more at freedom and ease under the protection of a great prince, and the same liberty would encourage the industrious trading part of the nation, who had been kept under by Penal Laws, to lay out their money, and promote universal trade, and by this means whatever we gained, they should infallibly lose.

This single consideration was powerful enough to invite them to study the most effectual means to obviate their own impoverishing, and having met with so favorable a conjuncture, as the aforementioned high boiling discontents of their own fomenting, they readily embraced the occasion to attempt something against the King.

It was easy to obtain the concurrence of the Prince of Orange, who besides the common interest with the States had that particular one of gratifying an ambition to have himself numbered among crowned heads, and to attain that crown in such a juncture, which by course of nature, the Prince of Wales being born, and more issue royal in prospect, he was not like to attain to.

But so daring and hazardous a design required some colorable pretext to give it countenance and hopes of success. Hence the glorious title of protector of the Protestant religion, and defender of English liberties was pitched upon as the most likely to bewitch the people here to embrace his knees; whereas if it were not for the instigations and interests before mentioned, I think none that know the religion of an Hollander would judge the Prince or States would be at the charge of a dozen fly boats, or herring busses to propagate it, or especially the Church of England as by law established. . . .

Let us inquire now into the liberties and freedoms the subjects enjoy in these countries the invaders come from, and compare them with our own and seriously consider whether they are more likely to continue us in the liberty we enjoy, or reduce us to the slavery and vassalage their subjects groan under: in some of which a servant, and boor's life, is scarce so valuable as that of their cattle; where no such thing as an English free-holder, or yeoman is known; where taxes as in Holland especially are set upon every smallest thing [that] is worn or eat, insomuch that you have five or six several excises for the ingredients of a soup; and you neither pass by land or water, but you pay an excise for it. Consider, I pray dear countrymen, these oppressions, and then think whether, for the empty name of securing Protestant religion, (which, as I shall hereafter show, neither is nor can be the design of the invaders) we should sell our birth-right for a mess of Dutch excised herb-pottage. . . .

. . . Let thinking men, and such as personally know the subjects of the King of England, who are embarked in this design, consider what they must expect from these men. They are either such as have fled from here to avoid the punishment due to seditious commonwealth men, open rebels, or inveterate haters of the monarchy and Church of England, or such as are men of broken and desperate fortunes.

Such as these are more likely to overturn our laws that they have so manifestly violated than to preserve them, are more like to be ravenous wolves, tigers and vultures than patriots and conservators of religion. Can those be true to the monarchy that have been in all the rebellions this kingdom has of late known, especially in the conspiracy of Shaftesbury,[37] and the rebellion of the Duke of Monmouth? Can such as are banished for rebellion and for enormous crimes, and have taken sanctuary and shelter in the United Provinces, and are infected with the witchcraft and contagion of rebellion against their lawful prince ever be like to maintain the sacred laws of the land? Can such be the protectors of our religion that were never known to have any more than outside show, who while they make long prayers that God would prosper them to destroy idolatrous worship, commit the highest sacrilege, and design not only to devour widows' houses, but already have divided among themselves the Estates of all such as they know are the most eminent in loyalty to the King, though those estates will not be sufficient to furnish every soldier with a competent demean, which we may be assured if they should succeed, they would never disband without. . . .

The rich citizens that have taken such a distaste to see a Romish chapel opened, though bettered from the expenses bestowed on that worship, must now give up their shops and warehouses to every Dutch petty tradesman, the richer merchants who, under the King's protection fetched the wealth of the Indies to the Royal Exchange, must now think themselves happy if they can be factors or very journey men to a Dutch peddler.

These come not to bring us rich commodities, but fire, sword, and the hands and claws of harpies. Consider, I pray you, oh! grave and

---

[37]Anthony Ashley Cooper, 1st Earl of Shaftesbury (1621–1683), Whig leader of the Exclusion Campaign (1679–81) to bar James.

rich citizens, what you shall barter with them. Do they offer you security of the Protestant religion? This you already enjoy, and may so without their carnal and cruel sword. What is it then you expect from them? Is it not much better that you are defended by the trained bands, a part of yourselves, and possessing your houses and stores? When your character was taken away, yet through the clemency of the King you enjoyed all the privileges of profit to yourselves, you had by your old one, only the governing part was put into some straighter subordination to the crown. But can you expect from conquerors that come for no other end but to seize on all your effects in trade and put them into Dutch bottoms and Dutch hands, such liberties as now you possess?

The plenty you enjoy has made you wanton, and while you have the government to take care of you and defend you from all dangers and destructions of traffic, you live in the affluence of all things. But though you now know by the intelligence and industry where the best markets are for buying and selling your commodities, can you think that if the Dutch accomplish their design they will permit you to have that freedom? No, self-interest will forbid all this. A new set of traders must fill the exchange and the up-shot of all must be whether the English or Dutch must enjoy the benefit of that trade our merchants have with so much advantage managed hitherto.

21

JOHN EVELYN

Diary Entries concerning France
1683–1684

John Evelyn (1620–1706) was a Restoration virtuoso. He was an essayist, a promoter of horticulture, and a great supporter of the new science as embodied in the Royal Society. He was a passionate Royalist during the interregnum. He was also a devout lay Anglican, counting a number

E. S. De Beer, ed., *Diary of John Evelyn* (Oxford: Clarendon Press, 1955), vol. 4, 331, 380. By permission of Oxford University Press.

of England's prominent clerics among his closest friends. He was com-
missioned by Charles II to write an anti-Dutch history of the Anglo-Dutch
War of 1672–74. However, in the 1670s, like many political moderates,
he came to believe that the Dutch threat was exaggerated. These diary
entries detail his thinking about France. In November 1688, his son,
John Evelyn Jr., took up arms in favor of William. Evelyn himself drew
up plans for a postrevolutionary regime.

July 15, 1683

The Turk likewise in hostility against the German Emperor, almost
master of the Upper Hungary, and drawing towards Vienna. On the
other side, the French (who 'tis believed brought in the infidel) disturbing their Spanish and Dutch neighbors, and almost swallowed all
Flanders, pursuing his ambition of a fifth and universal monarchy; and
all this blood and disorder in Christendom had evidently its rise from
our defections at home, in a wanton peace, minding nothing but luxury, ambition, and to procure money for our vices. To this add our
irreligion and atheism, great ingratitude, and self-interest; the apostasy of some, and the suffering the French to grow so great, and the
Hollanders so weak. In a word, we were wanton, mad, and surfeiting
with prosperity; every moment unsettling the old foundations, and
never constant to any thing. The Lord in mercy avert the sad omen,
and that we do not provoke him 'till he bear it no longer!

May 28, 1684

Now was Luxemburg rendered to the conquering French, which
makes him master of all the Netherlands, gives him entrance into Germany, and a fair game for an universal monarchy; which that we
should suffer (who only and easily might have hindered) all the world
were astonished at. But thus is the poor Prince of Orange ruined, and
this nation and all the Protestant interest in Europe following, unless
God of His infinite mercy (as by a miracle) interpose, and that our
great ones alter their counsels.

22

An Anti-French Tract

1686

Because of intense diplomatic pressure from the French ambassador in England, tracts critical of French policies were suppressed during James II's regime. However, this pamphlet, almost certainly printed in the Netherlands, was widely distributed in 1686. Its arguments were not new, repeating and updating claims advanced since the 1670s. At that time many in England began to feel that France had replaced Spain as the greatest threat to European peace. Contemporaries asserted that Louis XIV sought a "universal monarchy." A wide variety of English men and women repeated these claims in coffeehouses and in private correspondence.

Henry VIII, King of England, did, in his time, cause a medal to be stamped with a hand stretched out of a cloud, holding a balance in equal poise, whereof both the scales represented Spain and France, with this motto, *cui adhaero praest:* my alliance weighs it down. It seems that Prince well knew his own might; whereas now England may be compared to an ox, who being insensible of his own strength, quietly submits himself to the yoke. Evident it is, that England has many advantages beyond other kingdoms, but especially this: that being an island, it can easily secure itself against any foreign force; they that intend an invasion against it must be obliged to cross the seas and struggle with the winds and waves, and all the hazards and dangers of that unstable element, besides a very potent fleet, which alone is sufficient to deter the hardiest enemy from any such design. Now this being so, it is manifest that the King of England (having peace and a strict alliance with Holland) can over-balance the party he designs against.

This is a truth France is so fully convinced of that, notwithstanding the great antipathy there is between both nations, he has hitherto spared nothing, and is still turning every stone, to take off England

The Designs of France against England and Holland (1686), 1–2, 7.

from its true interest and to engage it on his side, or at least oblige it to stand neuter and to be an idle unconcerned spectator of the horrid tragedy the French King acts upon the theatre of Europe, because he well knows that England is better able to prevent it, and spoil his sport, than any other state or kingdom whatsoever, and rescue Europe from the universal slavery he prepares for it.

Would the King of England only be pleased to open his eyes, fast closed with the enchanted slumbers of the French Delilah, to take a view of his own strength and true interest, he should soon find himself making another figure amongst the princes of Europe, than of later years he has done, and with ease mount that high degree of power and glory, of being the professed umpire of the universe, the sovereign mediator and decider of controversies and the giver of peace to all Europe, which France, in a vain bravado, pretends to, when indeed he is the sole troubler of it.

To arrive at this transcendent pitch of grandeur and authority, two things only (which the King of England may do when he pleases) are requisite. The first is, that His Majesty do comport himself so, as to engage the love of his people and keep a right understanding between him and his Parliament. And the second, that he enter into a strict alliance with Holland, living in sincere amity, perfect union, and good correspondence with them in order to their common defense and security. The former of these is very easy, and the King will do it as soon as he shall resolve to desire nothing of his Parliament, but what is agreeable with the laws of the realm, which by his coronation oath he is obliged to observe and maintain; and the latter will be found to be of absolute necessity, as soon as the King of England shall please to stop his ears to the false suggestions of France and stifle those jealousies and resentments which his emissaries daily buzz into his head, there being nothing to fear for England from the States [Dutch Republic], whose desire is not to enlarge their dominions (as France does) by invading those of their neighbors, but only to keep what God has given them, and to maintain their subjects in the liberty they now enjoy. . . .

. . . All the world was in expectation of great things from His Majesty; his courage put all Europe in hopes of an universal relief, and some respite for Spain, but how has he frustrated and befouled their hopes, while his sole study is to please the Jesuits and to kindle a fire in his own kingdom, which probably he will never be able to quench when he would, as long as he dares not convene a free Parliament.

23

A Call for War against France

April 19, 1689

This printed tract reproduced a House of Commons committee address in support of war against France. While the address had widespread support in the House of Commons, this printing was unauthorized. A few weeks later, England declared war against France.

We, your Majesty's most loyal subjects the Commons of England in Parliament assembled, have taken into our most serious consideration the condition and state of this nation in respect to France and foreign alliances, in order to which, we have examined the mischiefs brought upon Christendom in late years by the French King who without any respect to justice has by fraud and force endeavored to subject it to an arbitrary and universal monarchy.

In prosecution of this design, so pernicious to the repose and safety of Europe, he has neglected none of those means, how indirect so ever, which his ambition or avarice could suggest to him. The faith of treaties among all princes, especially Christian princes, ever held most inviolable, has never been able to restrain him, nor the solemnest oaths to bind him, when any occasion presented itself for extending the limits of his kingdom, or oppressing those whom his interest inclined him to qualify by the name of his enemies. Witness his haughty and groundless declaration of war against the States General of the United Provinces in the year 1672, in which he assigned no other reason for disturbing that profound peace, which through God's mercy all Europe enjoyed at that time, but his own glory and his resolution to punish the Dutch for some imaginary flights and disrespects which he would have had the world believe they had put upon him. Whereas the true occasion of that war was nothing else but a formed design laid down and agreed upon by that King and his accomplices for the subversion of the liberties of Europe, and for abolishing the commonwealth of Holland as being too dangerous an example of liberty to the

---

An Address Agreed Upon at the Committee for the French War, and Read in the House of Commons (London, 1689), 1–2, 4–6.

subjects of neighboring monarchs. The zeal for Catholic religion, which was pretended by him in this and the following wars, did afterwards sufficiently appear to the world, to be no other than a cloak for his immeasurable ambition. For at the same time when the persecution grew hottest against the Protestants of France, letters were intercepted (and published) from him to Count Teckely,[38] to give him the greatest encouragement and promise him the utmost assistance in the war, which in conjunction with the Turk he then managed against the first and greatest of all the Roman Catholic princes. . . .

And as if violating the treaties and ravaging the countries of his neighbors' states were not sufficient means of advancing his exorbitant power and greatness, he has constantly had recourse to the vilest and meanest arts for the ruin of those whom he had taken upon him to subdue to his will and power, insinuating himself by his emissaries under the sacred name and character of public ministers into those who were entrusted in the government of kingdoms and states, suborning them by gifts and pensions to the selling their masters and betraying their trusts, and descending even to intrigues by women, who were sent or married into the countries of diverse potent princes to lie as snakes in their bosoms to eat out their bowels, or to instill that poison into them which might prove the destruction of them and their countries, of which Poland, Savoy and Spain, to mention no more at present, can give but too ample testimonies.

The insolent use he has made of his ill-gotten greatness has been as extravagant as the means of procuring it, for this single instance of Genoa may suffice, which, without the least notice or any ground of a quarrel whatsoever, was bombarded by the French fleet, and the Doge and four principal Senators of that free state constrained in person to humble themselves at that monarch's feet, which in the style of France was called chastising sovereigns for casting umbrage upon his greatness.

His practices against England have been of the same nature, and by corrupt means he has constantly and with too much success endeavored to get such power in the court of England, in the time of King Charles the Second and the late King James, as might by degrees undermine the government and true interest of this flourishing kingdom.

[38]Imre, Count Thokoly (1657–1705), known to the English as Emery, Count Teckely. A Hungarian rebel of a noble Protestant family, he conspired with the Ottomans against the Holy Roman Emperor in order to procure for himself a kingship in Hungary or a principality in Transylvania. He was known to have been in correspondence with the French court.

Another art which he has used to weaken England and subject it to his aspiring designs, was never to admit an equal balance of trade, nor consent to any just treaty of settlement of commerce, by which he promoted our ruin at our own charge.

When, from a just apprehension of this formidable growing power of France, the nation became zealous to right themselves—and the House of Commons, in the year 1677, being assured they should have an actual war against France, cheerfully raised a great sum of money, and an army as readily appeared to carry on the war—that interest of France had still power enough to render all this ineffectual, and to frustrate the nation of all their hopes and expectations.

Nor did France only render this desired war ineffectual, but had power enough to make us practice their injustice and irregularities (some years before) by turning our force against our next neighbors by assaulting their Smyrna fleet.[39]

Nor were they more industrious by corrupt means to obtain this power, than careful, by the same ways to support it; and knowing that from Parliaments only could probably proceed an obstruction to their secret practices, they attempted to make a bargain that they should not meet in such a time, in which they might hope to perfect their designs, of enslaving the nation.

In the same confidence of this power, they violently seized upon part of Hudson's Bay, and when the matter was complained of by the Company, and the injury offered to be proved, the best expedient France could find to cover their injustice and prevent satisfaction was to make use of their great interest in the Court of England to keep it from ever coming to be heard.

The French King, in pursuance of his usual methods of laying hold of any opportunity that might increase his power and give disturbance to others, has now carried on an actual war in Ireland, sending there a great number of officers with money, arms and ammunition, and, under the pretense of assisting the late King James, he has taken the government of affairs into his hands by putting all officers into commands and managing the whole business by his ministers, and has already begun to use the same cruelties and violence upon your Majesty's subjects, as he has lately practiced in his own dominions, and in all other places, where he has got power enough to destroy.

Lastly, the French King's Declaration of War against the crown of Spain is wholly grounded upon its friendship to your Majesty's royal

[39]Ships trading with the Ottoman Empire.

person, and no other cause of denouncing war against it is therein alleged than the resolution taken in that court to favor your majesty, whom he most injuriously terms usurper of England, an insolence never enough to be resented and detested by your Majesty's subjects.

After our humble representation of all these particulars to your majesty, if your Majesty shall think fit to enter into a war against France, we humbly assure your Majesty that we will give you such assistance in a Parliamentary way as shall enable your Majesty to support and go through the same. And we shall not doubt, but by the blessing of God upon your Majesty's prudent conduct, a stop may be put to that growing greatness of the French King, which threatens all Christendom with no less than absolute slavery, the incredible quantity of innocent blood shed may be revenged, his oppressed neighbors restored to their just rights and possessions, your Majesty's alliances and the Treaty of Nijmegen[40] supported to that degree, that all Europe in general, and this nation in particular may forever have occasion to celebrate your majesty and the opposer and overthrower of all violence, cruelty, and arbitrary power.

[40]Peace of Nijmegen (1678–79), in which England agreed to enforce the boundaries established by a pan-European diplomatic team. Louis XIV almost immediately violated the treaty, but neither Charles II nor James II sought to enforce the treaty.

24

JAMES WELLWOOD

Newspaper Account of Public Animosity toward France

October 30, 1689

The widely read newspaper, Mercurius Reformatus, *was written in large part by the moderate Whig doctor James Wellwood (1652–1727). The newspaper was widely distributed throughout England and had a very long run for a seventeenth-century newspaper.*

James Wellwood, *Mercurius Reformatus*, October 30, 1689, 2.

England, for these twenty years past, has been groaning after a war with France, and the constant grievance of the nation has been that the so much jealous friendship between our two last kings and Louis XIV obstructed a rupture with that crown. Now we have our wishes: our King has declared war against France, our old enemies, and has done it so that he has engaged the most considerable potentates of Christendom to bear a share with him in it, our Parliament have consented, and not only by a posterior act, but have advised His Majesty to it before the war was actually declared, so that this war is not so much properly the King's as ours; a war we longed for, the obstruction whereof we laid at the door of our two last kings, as one of our greatest grievances.

Revolution in Political Economy

Debates about political economy usually do not figure in accounts of the Revolution of 1688–89. This is, in part, because it is assumed that there was little disagreement about such matters until well into the eighteenth century. However, this assumption overlooks the activities and interests of James II and his opponents, as well as the growing prominence of political economic discussions among the English public. James, while still Duke of York, served as director of the Royal African Company and took an active interest in the East India and Hudson's Bay Company. And he was likewise keenly interested in imperial matters, particularly those related to North America and the West Indies. After all, it was a group of James's close associates who were responsible for seizing New Amsterdam from the Dutch in the 1660s and renaming it after their patron as New York. Moreover, by the 1680s, considerations of political economy had passed beyond the narrow confines of the court. There was a wide variety of literature available on economic and colonial matters. One enterprising man, John Houghton, had begun publishing a periodical devoted exclusively to economic issues.

25

Establishing Principles of Trade
in East India Company v. Sandys
1685

The seminal court case of East India Company v. Sandys *established the principles on which James II built his political economic regime. The case dealt with some difficult and technical legal issues. However, the basic questions being asked were straightforward: Was foreign trade the province of the king alone, or of the king in conjunction with Parliament? Did England's economic welfare depend on manufactures and foreign trade, or was England economically self-sufficient? The decision set a precedent that affected not only the East India Company, but also the Royal African Company and all of England's foreign trading concerns. The Lord Chief Justice, George Jeffreys, would soon become James II's Lord Chancellor. He remained a close adviser of the king until the revolution. He died in prison soon thereafter.*

The Argument of the Lord Chief-Justice Jefferies, at the Court of King's Bench, concerning the Great Case of Monopolies

The East India Company, Plaintiffs, and Thomas Sandys, Defendant; wherein their patent for trading to the East Indies, exclusive of all others, is adjudged good. . . .

First, then, to consider the difference between the inland and the foreign trade allowed of in our books, and that the king's prerogative does affect both. As to manufactures, under which all sorts of artificers are concerned, I think they remain with the most liberty by the common law; and as Mr. Attorney observed, the public weal is little concerned therein, only to preserve every one in the quiet enjoyment of the fruits of his own labor and industry. . . .

2. As to the trade of merchandise or inland commerce, generally speaking, it had the next freedom by the common law, but was subject nevertheless to be limited or restrained by the king's prerogative in

---

"East India Company v. Sandys," from T. B. Howell, comp., *A Complete Collection of State Trials,* vol. 10 (London: T. C. Hansard, 1816), 519, 523–24, 526, 528–29, 532–35.

several particulars; as for instance, to prevent all forestalling and engrossing. So Mr. Attorney did well observe, that numbers of people could not meet to traffic or merchandize, without being in danger of being punished as unlawful assemblies: the crown therefore granted the liberties of fairs and markets, for the sake of commerce and trade; all which did originally proceed from the crown, and therefore by abusing those liberties may still be forfeited to the crown. . . .

And here I must premise, that as at first all things were promiscuously common and undivided to all, so the free exercise of this universal right, was then instead of property; but as soon as the number of men increased, and they found by experience the inconveniency of holding all things in common, things were reduced into property by agreement and compact; either express, as by partition; or implied, by "premier occupancy."

After this government was established, and laws were made, even for the ordering those things to which no man had any right; as for example, deserts, places uninhabited, islands in the seas, wild beasts, fishes, and birds; the former were usually gained and disposed of by him that had the sovereignty over the people; the latter, by him that had the dominion over the lands and waters, who might forbid others from hunting, fishing, &c.

And in virtue of this universal law, his majesty and his predecessors have always disposed of the several plantations abroad, that have been discovered or gained by any of their subjects, and may do for the future, in case any other be discovered and acquired. For though the laws of nations can command nothing which the law of nature forbids, yet they may bound and circumscribe that which the law of nature leaves free, and forbid that which naturally may be lawful.

. . . [T]he Parliaments have in all ages even to this king's reign, since his restoration, thought fit to make more laws to prohibit foreign trade, than to increase it; as looking upon it more advantageous to the common weal. And thus having observed that other nations, as well as we, have not only thought it legal, but necessary, to make laws for the restraint of trade; and thereby thought they did no injustice to the liberty of mankind. . . .

The king is absolutely master of war and peace; which he could not be, in case he had not a power to lay restraint upon his own subjects in relation to foreign commerce; since [when] war is proclaimed, all public commerce is prohibited: and the counsel that argued for the defendant, admitted that the king might prohibit his subjects to go or trade beyond the seas in cases of wars or plagues. How strangely preposterous then would it be for a man to imagine, that the king should have an absolute power of war and peace, and yet be denied the means to preserve the one, and prevent the other! Is not that therefore the great reason why the king is at so great expense in maintaining ambassadors and envoys in all the trading parts of the world, without which we should be in a perpetual state of war? Would it not be monstrous, that then the king is entered into league with any sovereign prince, in a matter of trade very advantageous to his people, to have it in the power of any one of his subjects to destroy it? As for instance, suppose a league between our king and the emperor of Morocco, for a trade to Tangier, were made upon condition, that no English ship coming there for commerce, should be above a hundred tons, and a fleet of merchant ships within that condition, were in port at Tangier; and Mr. Sandys, with the same obstinacy as he seems to appear in this case, should have gone with a ship of above a hundred tons to Tangier; that would have been an absolute breach of the league; we should have been immediately in a state of war, the merchant ships and goods absolutely forfeited to the emperor by the law of nations, and they and their families thereby undone, without any remedy, 'till Mr. Sandys should be pleased to return to England; and also bring with him an estate sufficient to make them a recompense: and then also perhaps it would be difficult to contrive such an action in our law, to compel Mr. Sandys to do it. Besides, the king has no other way, if his ambassadors and ministers in foreign parts cannot prevail that right should be done to his subjects; or if Mr. Sandys's interloping ship, and all its cargo, had been wrongfully taken away from him by any foreign prince, but by the king's declaring of a war, and compelling them to make restitution by force; the consequence whereof will affect more than foreign traders, who would be then concerned, both in their persons and purses; and it would be very hard for all the king's subjects to lie under the burden and charge, and the profits and advantages accrue only to a few. . . .

. . . [F]or it is more for the king's benefit than it can be for his subjects, the greater the importation of foreign commodities is; for from thence arise his customs and impositions, those necessary supports of the crown: and therefore, in some sense, the king is the only person truly concerned in this question; for the island supported its inhabitants in many ages without any foreign trade at all, having in it all things necessary for the life of man.

. . . I think, if at this day most of the East India commodities were absolutely prohibited, though it might be injurious to the profit of some few traders, it would not be so to the general of the inhabitants of this realm. And therefore, as I have offered these few instances to prove the king should have such a prerogative; in the next place I come to show, that the kings of England have exercised this their prerogative in all ages: and as the king has the power of restraint of the foreign trade, so he is only judge when it is proper to use that power, which seems plainly to be for the same reason....

... But it has been too much practiced at this and other bars in Westminster Hall, of late years, to captivate the lay-gens,[41] by lessening the power of the king, and advancing, I had almost said the prerogative of the people: and from hence comes the many mischiefs to the king's subjects in parts abroad, by making the power of the king thought so inconsiderable, as though he were a mere duke of Venice, being absolutely dependant upon his parliament. Would it not be mightily for the honor and dignity of the crown of England, think you, that the emperor of Fez and Morocco, or any prince of the remote parts of the world, should be told, that Mr. Sandys, one of the king of Great Britain's subjects, came into the emperor's territories against his prince's consent, and that he had no power to hinder him, unless he would consult with all his nobles, and the representatives of all his common subjects, to assist therein? Would not the emperor believe Sandys to be the greater prince of the two? But though such sort of declamations are so much for the service of the crown, and for the honor of the kingdom, as they would have it believed; yet I think they have the same tendency of duty and service to the king, with some other matters that of late have happened amongst us, viz. Some have been so concerned, as well for the safety and security of his majesty's sacred person, and to make him formidable to his rebellious subjects at home, as to desire that his guards might be discharged, because it looked as though he designed to rule by a standing army; and to show their tenderness to his sacred life, would have him removed from the assistance of evil counselors as they called them; and put himself into the hands of assassins, as though one murdered prince were not sufficient to satisfy that piece of state policy in one and the same age. And in order that he might have sufficient [resources] to support the necessity, as well as the dignity of the crown, which all good subjects are zealous for; some, of late, have industriously endeavored to have prevented him from being able to borrow any money upon the credit of any part of his revenue, a privilege that the meanest of the persons

[41] Laypeople.

concerned in that question would think themselves highly injured to be debarred of.

These and the like attempts, if not prevented, will render the king and his government low and despicable in all other parts of the world. . . . I cannot help being of opinion, that his kingdom was in greater regard abroad, and the inhabitants thereof more prosperous at home when the prerogative of the crown was more absolute than now it is; therefore it is our duty as good judges, as well as good subjects, to endeavor to support it as much as we can by law.

26

JOSIAH CHILD

A Tory's Thoughts on Political Economy
1681

Sir Josiah Child (1630–1699) was one of the most prominent English merchants of the late seventeenth century. Child became involved in the East India trade in the 1650s, rising to be a director of the East India Company in 1674 and governor in 1681. From 1683, he was the main driving force behind the company. He became associated with Tory political circles in the early 1680s and was a close adviser of James II on economic matters. After the revolution, he took a less visible, but no less significant, role in company affairs. He was both a passionate defender of the company's privileges and a bitter opponent of the Bank of England. The pamphlet excerpted here was one of the many theoretical considerations of trade that Child published in his lifetime.

That trading merchants, while they are in the busy and eager prosecution of their particular trades, although they be very wise and good men, are not always the best judges of trade as it relates to the profit or power of a kingdom.

The reason may be because their eyes are so continually fixed, and

Josiah Child, *A Treatise* (London, 1681), 1–3, 6–9, 25–34, 38.

their minds intent, upon what makes for their peculiar gain or loss that they have not leisure to expatiate or turn their thoughts to what is most advantageous to the kingdom in general. . . . The like may be said of all shopkeepers, artificers, clothiers, and other manufacturers, until they leave off their trades and, being rich by the purchase of lands, become of the same common interest with most of their countrymen. . . .

That all domestic or foreign trade to any place or country that does not in the result and consequences of it increase the value of our English lands (the good plight whereof is the main basis of our wealth, freedom, and safety) ought not only to be discouraged, but totally rejected. . . .

I am of opinion the Dutch, nationally speaking, are the wisest people now extant for the contriving and carrying on their trades for the public advantage of their country. If any shall here object that if it be so, I am mistaken in my former notion that merchants are not always the best judges of trade, for the Dutch have the most merchants in their councils. The honorable Sir William Temple[42] has already answered for me that their councils are made up of very few or no trading merchants, but of civilians, or sons of merchants, that have long since left off their active trades, and have only now stocks in their East and West India companies, or in their banks . . . or other public funds.

. . . That though the dominion of the sea may be obtained by arms and fortunate battles at sea, it can never be retained, preserved, and maintained, but by the excess and predominance of foreign trade. . . .

That there is a necessity of a joint stock in all foreign trade where the trade must be maintained by force and forts on the land, and where His Majesty cannot conveniently maintain an amity and correspondence by ambassadors, and not elsewhere. . . .

6. All riches and power in nations, as well as private families, consists in comparison. A gentleman in the country may be accounted rich if he be much richer than other gentlemen, his neighbors, though but of moderate estate. So England may be said to be rich or strong, as our strength or riches bears a proportion with our neighbor nations, French, Dutch, etc. and consequently whatever weakens or depopulates them enriches and strengthens England. And most cer-

---

[42]Sir William Temple (1628–1699), ambassador to the Netherlands and author of a very influential analysis of the Dutch Republic, *Observations upon the United Provinces of the Netherlands.*

tain it is that no foreign trade does so work upon the manufactures of our neighbor nations as this trade of the East Indies. For the staple countries for silks and fine linen are Italy, France, Holland, Flanders, etc. insomuch as it is reasonably computed those countries, by the importation of East India silks and calicoes, not only into England but from England into their own countries, are abated in those fine manufactures above a million of pounds sterling per annum.

7. And which is a consideration of great weight, and may be of immense advantage to the strength, populousness and riches of this nation in a few years. England has already the principal trade of woolen manufactures, and now a quicker vent and export for them than ever it had in the memory of any man living. But throughout Christendom I have ever been of opinion that, generally speaking, there are more men and women employed in silk manufactures than in woolen, of which likewise England has obtained a considerable part considering the short time since our silk broad-weaving began.... And I am credibly informed the number of families already employed therein in England does amount to above 40,000. Now what should hinder but that in a few years more this nation may treble that number in such manufactures; since the East India Company has of late years found out a way of bringing raw silk of all sorts into this kingdom, cheaper than it can be afforded in Turkey, France, Spain, Italy, or any other place where it is made. Insomuch, as with East India silks we serve Holland, Flanders, and some other markets from England....

The Dutch, since the Portuguese sunk in the East India trade, have grown so potent in and by the trade of the Indies that they have, in three great and bloody wars, contended with us for the dominion of the sea, and yet secretly do not allow us the predominancy. Though they are not now at leisure to try the fourth war for it, yet if through the folly or madness of a few unthinking or self-interested men we should deprive ourselves of the trade of the East Indies (which God in mercy to England forbid), we should certainly save them the experiment of fighting with us the fourth time. They would carry the dominion of the sea clear and hold it forever, or until their commonwealth should be destroyed by land force or intestine broils.[43]

... If we should throw off the East India trade, the Dutch would soon treble their strength and power in India, and quickly subdue all other European nations in that trade, as they lately did the French,

---

[43]Civil wars.

notwithstanding their great strength at home, and have since, I hear, quarreled the Danes. By means whereof they would become the sole masters of all those rich and necessary commodities of the East, and make the European world pay five times more for them than they do, as they have already done by cloves, mace, cinnamon, and nutmegs, which would so vastly increase their riches as to render them irresistible. All wars at sea, and in some sense land wars, since the artillery used has become so chargeable being in effect but dropping of doits,[44] that nation that can spend most and hold out longest will carry the victory at last, with indifferent councils. If it be said, "where shall they have men?" I answer, if they have trade and money enough, they cannot want men. Seamen are inhabitants of the universe, and wherever they are bred, will resort to the best pay and most constant employment, especially in a country where they cannot be pressed or compelled into any service against their wills.

But it must be further considered that all the foreign trade in Europe does greatly depend upon East India commodities, and if we lose the importation of them into Europe we shall soon abate in all our other foreign trade and navigation, and the Dutch will more than proportionally increase theirs. The proportion of our decay and their increase, in such a case, would indeed be exactly the same, but that the excess of price which they would make the European world pay for East India commodities more than now they do would cause a disproportional and greater increase of their riches. The augmentation whereof would further enable them to overbalance us and all others, in trade, as well as in naval strength.

...The great increase of trade is not a constant and infallible consequence of the Protestant religion, because it proves not so in all Protestant countries. But whatever nation increases in the East India trade never fails proportionally to increase in other foreign trade and navigation. Secondly, admit that our reformation to the Protestant religion was one principal cause at first of our advance in trade and navigation, yet, now it is manifest that the increase of our trade and navigation is a great means, under God, to secure and preserve our Protestant religion: foreign trade produces riches, riches power, power preserves our trade and religion; they mutually work one upon and for the preservation of each other, as was well said by the late learned Lord Bacon, though in a different case, in his history of Henry the

[44] Small Dutch coins.

Seventh, that that King's fortune worked upon his nature, and his nature upon his fortune. . . .

A company in joint stock is a corporation by charter (and if it were by act of Parliament, it would be much better for the kingdom in general, as has been said) into which stock all the King's subjects, of what condition so ever, have at the foundation of it liberty to adventure what sum of money they please. The stock and trade is managed by a select council, or committee, consisting of a governor, deputy, and 24 committees chosen annually by the generality, in which every adventurer does not vote alike, but proportionally to his stock, viz. every 250 pound original stock has one vote; 500 pounds paid in has two votes, etc. After the first stock is settled, no man can come in but by purchase, which every Englishman has an equal liberty to do, and for which he pays nothing if he be a freeman, if not free, never above 5 pounds. . . .

Yet in regard that all other European nations do at this time trade there in joint stocks, is it not as great madness to enter raw and private persons against such compacted and united constitutions of experienced councilors as to fight a disordered undisciplined multitude against a well-governed veteran army supported with an inexhaustible treasure; or, as it is to imagine, as some men fondly do, that we can maintain and defend our Protestant religion against the Church of Rome without a national church in England. . . .

The East India Company of England, Holland, and all European nations that trade to India have power, by their charters, to make war upon any nation in India at their discretion, but not upon any European nation without His Majesty's consent. This power they must and ought to have for the well-carrying on of their trades. This power the English company have sometimes, but not often, exercised, but if it were not known in India that they have such a power, they should be continually affronted and abused by the natives. Now who shall this power be delegated unto in a regulated company? To all Englishmen, or to a single ambassador, or to many ambassadors and consuls?

27

CAREW REYNELL

A Whig View of Foreign Trade

1685

Despite Josiah Child's enormous power and influence, he did not monopolize economic thinking in the late seventeenth century. Since the 1650s, there had been a vigorous debate about the economy. By the 1680s, that debate had become highly politicized. This pamphlet, written by economic writer Carew Reynell, was typical of the Whig position. Little is known about Reynell.

Great Britain is acknowledged by all the world to be the Queen of the Isles, and as capable to live within itself as any nation, having not only all things necessary for the life of man, but also abundance of materials and store of manufactures and commodities to a superfluity for transportation, and is so incomparably situated that trade offers itself to all its ports and harbors. The soil of the country rich, abounding with much grain, horses, beefs, and sheep that wear the golden fleece, and other traffic; also mines of tin, lead and sea-coal inexhaustible; and no nation in the universe but partakes of its woolen manufactures. Its seas everywhere filled with shoals of fish that are as good as ready silver to fetch in all manner of foreign commodities. Now it is a very hard case if the heavenly bounty shall by nature thus furnish us with so great assistances that we should not add to it and give some advance by our own art and industry, bringing in whatever foreign arts, trades or husbandries may be profitable to us, for doubtless we may aggrandize our trade, to an inestimable account, if we would ourselves, and make our territories as rich and populous as we please under so glorious a King and government as we have. Had we but that public spirit as we ought, and gave countenance to brave actions and industrious men, and minded the business of trade and populacy as much as we do pleasures and luxury. Get first but trade and

Carew Reynell, *A Necessary Companion or the English Interest Discovered and Promoted* (London: William Budden, 1685), 1–3, 12–15, 17–18, 48, 60–61.

people which will produce riches, and then pleasure will come of course. Riches are the convenience of the nation; people are the strength, pleasure, and glory of the nation, but trade preserves both. And if we be but industrious no nation can exceed us either in a home or foreign trade.

. . . I have hinted here at the chief advancements we are capable of, and those I am sure will do the work effectually if encouraged; for though we are a nation already pretty substantial, yet it's easy for us to be ten times richer, and that in the third part of an age, if we will set aside some portion of our time and money, for public actions and such contrivances that may be for the general good. . . .

All of us both country and city should be endeavoring, how they may do good in their generation, and be beneficial to the public: For if we were once full of people and full of trade, rents of lands would quickly raise, the King's revenue would be greater, the nobility and gentry richer, the commonalty more substantial, and the poor be all employed to advantage. We want people, and yet as the case stands we want means to maintain them; when if we please, we may increase our people by multitudes, and grow infinitely rich by them too: For it is a sad case there should be so many lusty poor about everywhere, and yet so many manufactures want to be brought in, which would set at work millions of people more than we have to spare. For it is manufactures must do the work, which will not only increase people, but also trade, and advance it. It saves likewise money in our purses by lessening importation, and brings money in by exportation. . . .

The happiness and welfare of all people arises, by having or acquiring, through some industry or other, such conveniency of livelihood as may not only keep them from want and poverty, but render them pleasant and sociable to one another. This holds both in private persons and families, and also in bodies politic, that they may be able to grow and flourish, at least bear up against the malignity of enemies and adverse fortune. . . .

For it is not all trading [that] advantages a nation. A people may be undone by some kind of merchandise, for many merchants, so they advantage themselves, care not what injury they may do to the public. . . . And to the East Indies we carry nothing but ready money, and bring in again nothing worth anything but spices, and though the pretense is that those things so imported, when exported, bring in more money than they carried out. Yet we find the money decays, and they bring in little money with them, only still more superfluity of wines, silks and unnecessary toys. But it were well if we could manage the East India trade as the Dutch do, who carry no silver from Holland, but drive the trade with the silver they get from Japan in exchange for other commodities they bring to them, which we may do in a better and speedier way than they can, if permitted by the means of the West Indies (the Isthmus of Panama being within one hundred and sixty leagues off Jamaica, and but six weeks sail from Japan), and driving the West and East India trade under one voyage, carry what silver we will from the West Indies there if it is required, and so come back here with East India goods and West India silver. . . .

Trade and populousness of a nation are the strength of it, and the product of it is riches. Money, trade, and populousness are by all means possible to be kept in a nation; the more populous, the more trade; the more trade, the more populous, and the more trade and population, the more money.

But then trade must be regulated, for if a nation pursue either but one or few trades, populacy may be lost for want of a variety of trades to employ men, for they will go to other countries where there is more trade, and thus trade will decay for want of people. And so in the end people and trade will decay, as here in England, both which we may easily remedy. . . .

Where abundance of manufacturing people are, they consume and sweep away all country commodities and the wares of ordinary retail trades, with all sorts of victuals, wearing apparel, and other necessaries, and employ abundance of handicraftsmen, in wooden and iron work for tools and instruments that belong to their trades, and so maintain and increase abundance of husbandmen, retailers, and artificers of all sorts, and they, again increasing, take up more manufactures, and so they thrive one by another, *ad infinitum*. . . .

Another way for increasing populacy is by encouraging all sorts of trading people to come and inhabit here, which is done by making all nations free denizens that will live here. And why should not we, as the Hollanders do at Amsterdam, declare all the world to have freedom in our nation as their own? It would make us thrive infinitely, and bring in all the arts, manufactures, and ingenuity of Europe. Some object they would breed a mixed nation. As for that they would signify nothing as to the number of our own. If it did, why may not several nations live under one government, as they do in Holland? Trading people value not that, they love to live where they are most secure; besides, coming in by degrees they would not be considerable. And generally they that come over are men that would marry English women, so are English·presently, and are good preferment to ordinary women, being generally tradesmen and manufacturing men, as we see in many French and Dutch already, that are perfectly English. However, in half an age they would be as much English as ourselves. The old stock going off, and the children being born in England, supplying their places; and however at present live as quietly, and are good subjects, and as great lovers of us and the kingdom as others, or else they would never leave their own nation, so formerly to inhabit here. For all that do so leave their country show an extraordinary affection unto this place, and so are by all means to be received and countenanced. Whatever they are before, when once they come here, to be under our laws, customs, and government, they are soon all one with us.

28

An Early Defense of the Bank of England

1694

Parliament created the Bank of England, England's first government-backed bank, in April 1694. Although private bankers had existed in England for a long time, the directors of the Bank of England initiated an informational campaign to explain the new institution to potential investors. The bank, which had close links to the Whig Party, had powerful enemies in its early years. Some of these, including many members of the East India Company, tried to create a rival Land Bank. That bank failed in 1696. The pamphlet excerpted here was one of many printed in the early years of the Bank of England. The author has never been convincingly identified.

This Royal Bank of credit will be able to issue out bills of credit to a vast extent, that merchants will accept of, rather than money. Most merchants in Europe when they know the manner how the security of this fund is settled by Act of Parliament (it not being in the power of the Bank Corporation to injure any foreigner or native), it will encourage

HM, *England's Glory; or, The Great Improvement of Trade in General, by a Royal Bank* (London: T. W., 1694), 7–14, 18–36.

them to accept of these bills rather than money; the fund being unquestionable, and no Security in Nature better; their Bills being more safe, portable, & transferable than money, and better than cash in the chest, as gold is better than silver: men may be robbed of money in specie, and there is great trouble in the carrying and recarrying it. Now a bank bill is free from all these troubles, and has advantages beyond gold or silver. . . .

Now every man's money is as safe in this bank, as his cash in his own chest, where it lies and pays him no interest, 'till he lends it out or lays it out; this he may be with his money and credit in the bank, as soon as he can: if any desires to leave his money in this office, it may be upon such terms, as the office shall propose; none are forced to it, nor urged to it, unless they think that they can get by it.

These bills of credit will be transferable; men may transfer their credit from one to another at the office, and also at a distance, if they will run the risk of counterfeiting the bill. They may assign their interest in the office, so far as the bill goes, to whom they please, who shall have the same right of receiving the money, as the party had to whom it was first given. And for the security of all who shall lodge money in the bank, the whole estate of the corporation, payable out of the Exchequer, as the Act directs, is liable to make good all the acts and miscarriages of the Office of Bank, which is an unquestionable security to all that deposit money in these banks. . . .

Obj[ection]. 2. We make more goods than we can consume, or the world will utter.

Ans[wer]. People will increase, for trade will bring in people as well as riches to the nation: where trade is, there will be employment; where employment is, there will people resort; where people are, there will be consumption of all commodities. These banks being once settled, trade will flourish; the Dutch, French, and Flemish, and people from all parts of Europe that have estates, or can raise money, will resort hither to enjoy themselves and their estates, under so gracious and indulgent a King and Queen. It is not a contemptible consideration, that these Banks will be great satisfaction and security to the nation, while all the world that trades with us, will have kindness for us; especially when these banks keep their money. They will do all they can to preserve their cashiers, lest they should lose their estates, having nothing but a bill of credit for it. I appeal for the confirmation of this to all those that had credit upon the Bank of Amsterdam, what thoughts they had, when the French King was near those gates? And whether they would not have diverted him, had it been in their power. Pray God he come not there again.

Obj[ection]. 3. We have too many people already.

Ans[wer]. It is evident that the riches of a kingdom, are the people of the nation; lands are at a greater rate, where people are numerous, as about London; but in America, where people are few, they are little worth: and this is true, that people unemployed are as caterpillars to plants, and worms to woods, that only waste the product of industrious hands.

I propose employment, and there is no doubt, that the consumption of the people is not so much, as the product of their labors, which is the real riches and strength of the nation; and the more the merrier, like bees in a hive, and better cheer too.

The Crown may be supplied with whatsoever is necessary, and the Prince may have whatsoever humane nature is capable of. In this great abundance, nothing will be reasonably denied to the King; only his hands will be tied with these silken cords, to keep that station the Constitution of this government has set him in.

A considerable share may, if the Parliament please, be ascertained to the Crown out of the clear profits. The Prince and people ought to grow together, else the body politic will be monstrous. Upon a sudden emergency here will be ready money to equip Armadas, provide armies, levy soldiers. And when there is leisure for deliberation, and that the Parliament and King judge it requisite, these Banks may be in a capacity to supply the Crown with whatever money it needs at a reasonable rate: suppose it should be a million, if the Bank be certainly repaid, this million in ten years, that is one hundred thousand pounds a year; the credit of the Bank is not impaired, and so in proportion any sum over or under this. How easily will taxes be borne; impositions are heavy when people are poor. But when rents rise, trade flourishes, and money is plentiful, a man that gets a hundred pounds a year, can better pay ten pounds, than he that gets but ten pounds a year, can pay ten shillings.

The benefits that accrue to the Crown in these and many more particulars, are very pleasant to reflect upon. O that reverence that all persons will have for such a Prince, that puts them into such a condition; and by this prudent management, keeps them in such a flourishing estate. When the people's yoke is lined with peace and plenty, it will make them cheerful under it, and not desirous to shake it off. If some few should surfeit and grow wanton, the generality of the people (being content in their condition) would certainly keep them in awe. Methinks the bees, by all possible means preserving their King, because their very being depends upon him, are a perfect emblem of a people honoring such a prince.

The people shall have advantages.

1. The poor.
2. The middle sort.
3. The rich.
4. The mariner.
5. The merchant, as has been fully shown already.

1. The poor have most need; I do not mean all shall be rich, but the able poor may be employed, and well paid for their work, their children brought up to learning and labor, and the nation freed from those rates (made in every parish to relieve the poor) which in many places begin to grow greatly burdensome, and which amounts to seven hundred thousand pounds per annum. But the honest ingenious poor will find friends to be security for them at the Bank.

2. The middle sort of people may be benefited; I mean small freeholders, farmers, and tradesmen; these will quickly increase their stocks by their honest industry; had they tools to work with, I mean, a plentiful stock to drive their trades with, and husband their lands, and keep their commodities for a market; all their defects may be supplied by the Bank, supposing them ingenious and industrious. The middle tradesmen so soon as they have made a piece or two of cloth or stuff, are forced to sell it at any rates, to put them in a capacity to provide new materials to keep themselves and dependents in action. At these banks they may take up money upon their goods, at the market price, 'till better times come.

3. Further, the gentry that in a frolic run themselves in debt, and in danger of ruining their families, and extirpating their names, and who formerly could not borrow four thousand pounds upon one thousand a year, without personal security of friends, besides mortgaging of their lands, may now borrow four thousand pounds upon three hundred a year. . . .

5. Infinite are the advantages of merchandising in general: a merchant has three thousand pounds stock, and brings a cargo of goods of that value into England, immediately he may have three thousand pounds at the Bank upon these goods, and pay the office as he sells them; and this he may do again, as often as he pleases; and with three thousand pound stock lay in fifteen thousand pounds worth of com-

modities, or goods. So that the stocks our merchants now use in England, may drive eight times the trade they now do. Between them and the Bank, if the Parliament will admit, they may engross the greatest part of the merchandise, will employ our ships; I might enlarge here to a volume but my design is only to give hint of the great advantages these banks will bring in to the nation.

. . . Now compare our banks with this; if our nation should be put hard upon by any foreign power, the King may have from these enough to supply his wants, the Parliament consenting and approving; and may tend to the overthrowing of our enemies by sea and land.

And in so great a necessity, should our banks be drained, if our country be saved, and our enemies defeated, the land will remain, and most of the money will be in the nation, and all creditors may have satisfaction by their bills of credit, being as useful as money, and may be gradually satisfied with money in specie, as it can be raised and paid into the Bank by the Exchequer: the Bank at Hamburg is much of the same nature with that at Amsterdam; only they keep their whole fund in specie, and so it is much worse, their money lying dead. Consider how money will abound in England, if five millions, or ten millions of ready money, and credit current (equivalent to money) should in a little time be added to the present stock of the nation. These banks probably will do all this and much more.

29

SLINGSBY BETHEL

A Whig View of Trade and Geopolitics
1680

Slingsby Bethel (1617–1697) was a powerful London cloth merchant and Whig politician. He was a religious Nonconformist and had served as sheriff of London from 1680 to 1681. He spent the entirety of James II's reign in exile in Hamburg and the Netherlands. While in the Dutch Republic, he was active in starting a cloth-manufacturing business. Bethel

Slingsby Bethel, *The Interest of Princes and States* (London, 1680), 1–4, 10–13, 57, 70.

returned to England in February 1689. His writings on trade and politics were printed in a variety of forms in the late seventeenth century.

Formerly the affairs of Christendom were supposed to be chiefly swayed by the two great powers of Austria (wherein Spain is understood) and France, from whom other princes and states derived their peace and war according to the several parties they adhered unto. But now the puissance of the former, being so much abated that it deserves no rank above its neighbors, France, of the two, remains the only formidable potentate, of whose greatness all princes and states are as much concerned to be jealous as formerly they were of that of Austria. . . .

The isle of Great Britain, of which England is the most considerable part, and that which is chiefly taken notice of in the world, having the advantage of an island in being divided from all other countries by the ocean, narrow and northern seas, is not subject to those incursions that contiguous countries are, not being in danger from abroad while its naval strength is preserved by keeping their shipping in good repair, and their mariners encouraged by good usage. Neither is it fit for foreign acquisitions, in regard of the uncertainty of wind and weather, and chargeableness of transportation; but contenting themselves with the bounds that providence has given them, making it their design to improve their advantage for trade, to increase their greatness at home, is their first domestic interest. For as self-defense is the chief interest of every creature, natural or politic, and as without trade no nation can be formidable, especially at sea, nor able to maintain a sufficient naval guard, or defend themselves against their powerful neighbors, so trade must be the principle interest of England. And this nature seems to admonish them unto, prohibiting their affecting foreign conquests by placing them with advantages as they are an island. . . . England has further the advantage of all other countries in some customs and practices: as in that of breeding the younger sons of gentlemen, and sometimes of nobility, to the ministry, law, trade, and physic,[45] without prejudice to their gentility, their heralds not requiring so much as any restoration in such cases, although it frequently falls out that gentlemen, during their apprenticeships to trades, come by the death of their elder brothers to be baronets, and

[45]Medicine.

sometimes barons. In which particular, England may well be said to come nearest unto ancient prudence and right reason of all other nations. For if no country can be rich or flourish without trade, as indisputably it cannot be more or less considerable but according to the proportion it has of commerce, and that anciently men were esteemed, honored and dignified according to the benefit and commodity their country had received by them, the traders of a nation ought to be most encouraged, and trade accounted the most honorable of all professions. Secondly, by their greatest nobility marrying with all degrees, where fortunes answer their qualities. . . . In Germany, Denmark, Sweden, and Poland it is esteemed below the quality of a gentleman to be bred to either trade, law, ministry, or physic: (except that among the Papists some are bred to the Church to get great estates that, leaving no known posterity, they may thereby advance their families as they many times do in Germany, Italy and other places). Neither will the greatest fortunes tempt them to marry into the families of any of these callings they choosing to live miserably, as many of them to do, rather than to match under their degree, or at least not into such as they esteem noble. . . .

Trade being the true and chief intrinsic interest of England, without which it cannot subsist, thus much could not well be avoided in the making out that as well by some constitutions and customs as by its native commodities and conveniences, it so far excels all other kingdoms and commonwealths in worldly advantages that providence may be said to have left nothing more for the people of England to do in order to their earthly felicity than desiring of it, the matter of trade being naturally so prepared and fitted for them, that it may even be a reproach to them not to advance trade, though no great glory to do it; nothing, except some accidents extraordinary, or violent obstructions, (as imposing upon conscience, etc.) or want of good laws, or the execution of them, being capable of hindering the increase of it. And now, as from the growth of trade there does naturally arise, not alone riches to the subject, rendering a nation considerable, but also increase of revenue, and therein power and strength to the Sovereign; so it is the undoubted interest of His Majesty to advance and promote trade by removing all obstructions and giving it all manner of encouragement.

As first, by lessening the over-great impositions upon native commodities and upon such as are necessarily imported to be manufactured in England, or to be again transported.

Secondly, by causing the native commodities to be faithfully and truly made and ordered.

Thirdly, by laying all companies open, or at least by leaving them free, for all to come into them that please, without fines, more than a small acknowledgment tying them in such case from burdening their own manufactures with taxes, as they usually do for the raising money to spend profusely and wantonly. What objections may be made against this general rule, in reference to the East India's joint stock, I know not; but this I am sure may be said for it: that the Hollanders, driving their East India trade by a joint stock, is no argument for England to do the same, for they, having the public purse of the company, purchased and conquered several countries and petty kingdoms, which engages them often in wars with their neighbors and necessitates them to keep up a standing militia of 30 or 40,000 men, with many garrisons, and 100 or more ships equipped as well for men of war at sea as for merchants use. The carrying on of such a government, and defraying the charge of it, is no otherwise feasible than by a society and joint stock, the maintaining of their propriety being impracticable by an open trade; but the case not being the same with England, they having nothing in propriety save the insignificant castle of St. George upon the coast of Cormandel, and the little island of Bombay, given them lately by the King. Their trade being all by factories, there is not that reason nor necessity upon them for a joint-stock, as upon Holland; and societies, in restraining the number, both of buyers of the native and sellers of foreign commodities, must consequently tend to the abating the price of the first, and enhancing the rate of the latter, nothing being more plain to reason than that the fewer buyers of native commodities, the cheaper they must be, as the fewer sellers of foreign, the dearer they must be, and that which abates the price of native commodities and raises the price of foreign must be against the interest of a nation. And therefore the Netherlanders, who certainly understand the interest of trade, equal to any people living, though by making the interest of trade matter of state, they have an eye of regulation upon it, yet admit of no restraining companies, as in England, except in their East and West India trades, where they have great possessions in propriety. . . .

Ninthly, banks (not bankers) but such as are in use at Venice, Amsterdam, and Hamburg, where the several states are secure, keeping particular accounts of cash for all men desiring it, are of great advantage to merchants and traders in securing their monies from many casualties, and making receipts and payments speedy and easy; besides, so certain, without the danger of losing acquaintances or by death, or otherwise to be in want of witnesses as takes away all occasions of suits about them, bank-accounts being allowed for undeniable testimonies in law, but of these, I confess there are no thriving and flourishing examples, save under republics. . . .

. . . The French are the only people in all the world that the English nation has cause to be jealous of, all other countries being incapable of putting them in danger. For though the Dutch have of late in their contests with them come (by accident) better off than they could well have hoped for, or formerly did, yet experience showed even then that they are not fit for land invasions; and that they can never agree with France, while they remain a republic, for a conquest of England (as some will irrationally suggest) may be relied upon; and not only in that they want people for such a design, but also because, being a country that has as many wise men among them as the world affords, they cannot promise themselves any security in a partnership with a prince so much too mighty for them as is the French King, and therefore we ought not to suffer groundless suggestions to turn us from our true interest in keeping of them up. . . .

. . . It could no way be the interest of England to ruin them, to the end to increase their own trade, because if their aims be only traffic, the world affords matter enough to satisfy both nations, and that England has so much the advantage of Holland in natural helps for trade that if they do but improve them, they cannot miss of exceeding all others in it; and if they will be careless of their common concerns, they ought not to draw an argument from their own neglects and sloth, for the envying other men's activity and diligence.

Revolution in the Church

Before 1689, all English men and women were required by law to attend Church of England services on Sundays. By the 1680s, the Church was deeply divided between defenders of the "high" and "low" church positions. High churchmen were in favor with Charles II and tended to be more religiously intolerant, more committed to divine-right monarchy, and less indulgent toward ritual divergence within the Church. Low churchmen, by contrast, tended to be religiously tolerant, committed to the notion that the form of government was determined by the nation and not by God, and were willing to accept diversity in ritual within the Church of England. James II, however, pursued ecclesiastical policies that were not easily compatible with either position. William and, especially, his wife, Mary, held views very close to the low church position. This section includes typical high and low church views, concluding with the key statement of James II's religious policies and the Nonconformist reactions to it.

30

GEORGE HICKES

Criticism of Religious Nonconformity

1685

George Hickes (1642–1715) was a prolific, influential, and controversial high church cleric of the late seventeenth century. He served as dean of Worcester in James II's reign. While his brother, James, was a Presbyterian divine, he himself was always virulent in his attacks on Nonconformity. He was also bitterly anti-Catholic. Hence during James II's reign, he was an outspoken critic of the king's ecclesiastical policies. He was, however, unable to stomach the revolution and refused the oaths to the new regime. He spent the remainder of his career as a bitter opponent of the postrevolution church.

There remains nothing then but to assert that you are punished for serving God, or for worshipping God in a way which you are sure is true. That you worship God in a true way, I verily believe, and could heartily join with you in other circumstances. But then you are not punished for worshipping God in that manner; for the same laws you complain of, allow you to worship God in what fashion you please; and not only you, but your family, be it as great as it will; and lastly, not only your family, but five persons more; which allowance, were you the only Christians in the world, and the magistrates heathens; or, which your friends are more likely to suggest, were they Papists or

George Hickes, *A Letter from a Person of Quality to an Eminent Dissenter* (London: T. B., 1685), 12–14, 18–24.

atheists, is so far from being persecution, that were you of the temper of the Primitive Christians, you would esteem it as a great privilege, and instead of reviling, thank the kind magistrate for the same. But then if on the contrary hand you be considered (and many good English men, and good Christians cannot but consider you) as a sort of men that have formerly raised a most unnatural rebellion, and now make schism in the Church, and broils in the state, the punishments you suffer and complain so loudly of, will be so far from seeming persecution of you as Christians, that they will rather seem your just dessert, as factious and turbulent subjects. And I assure you, that your brethren in France (whom you falsely so call, and for whom you pretend so great respect) are so far from judging you persecuted, that they will not excuse you; but wonder at your non-submission to the Church, and pity your mistakes, that make you stand out against the laws. They that have seen and examined our English Liturgy, which is printed at Geneva in French, cannot understand your notion of persecution. And Minister Claude,[46] the most famous of them all, for piety and learning, told me in the presence of many others, (after a discourse, wherein he said all for you that could be said) that he wondered how the Presbyterians in England could rend the peace of the Church, for such little indifferent matters; and that, if he were in England, he would be of the Episcopal party, and heartily submit himself to the discipline and government of the Church of England. And if you would do so too, how happy a thing would this be both for yourselves and the nation? Or seeing, as you pretend you cannot, yet at least live peaceably, and forbear to trouble the world with compassing sea and land; that is, by doing all that you can, like your fathers the old Pharisees, to make proselytes; when yet you cannot show any sinful condition of communion with the Church of England, nor prove your way of worship as apostolical, as that of hers; from which out of pride, interest or ignorance, or party altogether you dissent. I am sure this would rather become the dissenting brethren, then to foment divisions, raise parties, betake themselves to the wickedest of men, as of late to——and cry up the King's prerogative, which they formerly cried down; which with many other self-contradictions, confirms me in an opinion you know I was of before, that in those matters wherein you differ from us, you are men of no principles, and know not where to fix it. . . .

---

[46]Jean Claude (1619–1687), a French Protestant minister.

As for the Bill of Comprehension,[47] it begun to be talked of, before I left my country, and I have often discoursed with many of the projectors, but could never understand from them, how it was practicable to unite so many incompossible[48] sects, which agree in nothing, but their opposition to the Church. However if the altering, or taking away of a ceremony or two would effectually unite the Protestant parties, as you are pleased to assert, I think it would be worth the while to do it, and that the doing of it for so sure an end, would reflect no dishohor upon the Church of England, which acknowledges the few innocent and decent ceremonies, which she has ordained to be indifferent and alterable, according to the exigency of times. Neither, if this were done, could the Romish church have the least apparent reason to reproach us for such a slight alteration; seeing her own missals and breviaries have been so diverse and different in several times and places; and have undergone so many emendations, or rather corruptions, before they were established in the present form, by the authority of Pius V[49] and the decree of the Council of Trent.[50] But unless this alteration would surely and infallibly produce this effect, it had far better be let alone, and in the mean time, I would have all good Christians wait in peace and compliance with the established religion, 'till authority shall think to make this alteration in it, that so a poor English traveler would not be tauntingly asked by every impertinent priest here whether he were a true son of the Church, or Presbyterian, or Independent, or Anabaptist, or Quaker. And I assure you, when they meet with a man that owns himself a true son of the Church of England, they will seem with great formality to pity him more than any other; but yet they will never attempt to convert him. But when they meet with one that will own himself of any other sort, they will be pleased, smile in their sleeves, and set upon him as a person not far from their Kingdom of God. And I am persuaded, had you seen or heard as much of their idolatries, blasphemies and superstitions, as I have done in one Christmas, one Lent and one Easter, you would be so far from doing the Church of England any ill office, that you would rather (like

[47]Bills of Comprehension, proposed in 1668, 1678, and 1689, generally aimed at modifying the episcopal structure or liturgy of the Church of England in order to encompass Protestant Dissenters. None of these bills were successful.

[48]Incompatible.

[49]Pius V (r. 1566–72), a reform-minded pope whose pontificate oversaw the implementation of many of the tridentine reforms.

[50]Council of Trent (1545–63), the great council of the Roman Catholic Church that was convened to reform corruption and to confront the rise of Protestantism.

St. Paul after his conversion) preach against your own partisans, and thank God that you lived in a Church reformed from Romish idolatry and superstition. And I cannot but freely confess, that I am since my Travels become ten times a greater lover of our own Church and as many times a greater hater and detester of the Romish Church, than I was before. And therefore I cannot here dissemble the hearty grief I have conceived, for the great hopes you have, that the licenses (as you express it) will be once more authorized by his Majesty, or the Declaration revived.[51] . . . 'Tis that which the Roman Catholics here (especially the Priests) do hope, and wish for as well as you. They desire nothing more, than such a toleration, as that was, knowing that it must needs tend to the ruin of the Church of England, which is the principal butt of all their envy and malice; as being the main support and credit of the Reformed Religion everywhere, and the only hedge against popery itself in our unfortunate British Isles. We meet with not a few priests of several orders, that have the confidence (in our most familiar conferences) to tell us, that by the just judgment of God upon our Church, the time of her ruin is at hand; the nation itself being over-spread with schism and atheism, and the hearts of the faithful being disposed by the spirit and providence of God, to re-embrace the holy Catholic truth. And therefore they freely confess, that this time of distraction is their harvest; and withal express their intentions and zeal to transport themselves into England at the critical time of toleration, that they may be fellow-laborers with yourselves in that harvest.

[51]The Declarations of Indulgence were royal suspensions of penal laws against Roman Catholics and Protestant Dissenters; Charles II unsuccessfully issued two such declarations, in December 1662 and again in March 1672—both of which were vehemently rejected by Parliament. James II issued even more sweeping indulgences in 1687 to 1688.

31

GILBERT BURNET

Divisions within the Church

1713

Gilbert Burnet (1643–1715) was a well-known Scottish Episcopalian who associated with Whigs and low church religious groups. Late in his life, he took the occasion of the reprinting of his essay on pastoral care to add a new preface to the work. In it, he wrote a history of church divisions since the revolution, outlining the differences between high and low church as he understood them.

I will say nothing that may justly provoke any; but since I myself am ranked among the *Low Church-men,* I will open all that I know that is particular to them and then leave it to others to judge what reason can be given for entertaining such hard thoughts of them.

They are cordially and conscientiously zealous for the Church, as established by law: but yet they think no humane constitution is so perfect, but that it may be made better, and that the Church would be both more secure and more unexceptionable, if the administration of the discipline were put into other hands, and in a better method. They lay the foundation of all that they believe in the Christian religion in the Scriptures: these and these only are the measures and standard of their faith. No great names nor shows of authority overawe them: they search the Scriptures, there they seek and find their faith.

They think that in matters declared to be indifferent, no harm could follow on it, if some regard were had to the scruples of those who divide from us, in order to the fortifying the whole by uniting us among ourselves: but 'till that can be done, they think a kind deportment towards Dissenters softens their prejudices, and disposes them to hearken to the reasons which they can offer to them, with all the force they can, but without the asperity of words, or a contemptuous

From the "Preface" to Gilbert Burnet, *A Discourse of the Pastoral Care* (London: Daniel Midwinter and Benjamin Cowse, 1713).

behavior; in which they have succeeded so well, that they see no cause to change their conduct.

They do indeed make a great difference between Dissenters and Papists: they consider the one as a handful of people true to the Protestant Religion, and to our national interests, not capable of doing us much mischief, and who are, as far as appears to them, contented with their toleration, and are only desirous to secure and maintain it. They have another and a very different opinion of popery: they consider that Church not only with relation to the many opinions and practices held by them, such as transubstantiation, Purgatory, and the worshipping of saints and images, and a great many more: they are persuaded that these are false and ill grounded, but they could easily bear with them, as they do with other errors: but they consider popery as a conspiracy against the liberty and peace of mankind, on design to engross the wealth of the world into their own hands; and to destroy all that stand in their way, sticking at no practice, how false, base, or cruel soever, that can advance this. This is the true ground of their zeal against popery, and indeed against everything that has a tendency that way.

The pretending to an independency of the Church on the state, is not only in their opinion a plain attack made on the supremacy vested by law in the Crown, and a casting disgrace on our reformers, and on every step made in the Reformation, which are openly owned by the chief promoters of this new conceit: but it is a direct opposition to the same persons to serve other purposes, in the 13th of the *Romans, Let every soul be subject to the higher powers,* in which all subjects are equally comprehended. The laws of GOD are certainly of a superior obligation to any humane authority, but where these laws are silent, certainly all subjects of what sort soever, are bound to obey the laws of the land where they live.

The raising the power and authority of sacred functions, beyond what is founded on clear warrants in Scripture, is, they think, the readiest way to give the world such a jealousy of them, and such an aversion to them, as may make them lose the authority that they ought to have, while they pretend to that they have not.

They dare not un-church all the bodies of the Protestants beyond sea; nor deny to our Dissenters at home, the federal rights common to all Christians; or leave them to uncovenanted mercy. They do not annul their baptism, or think that they ought to be baptized again in a more regular manner, before they can be accounted Christians. They know of no power in a priest to pardon sin, other than the declaring the Gospel pardon, upon the conditions on which it is offered. They know of no sacrifice in the Eucharist, other than the commemorating that on the cross, with the oblation of the prayers, praises, and alms-giving, prescribed in the office. They are far from condemning private judgment in matters of religion: this strikes at the root of the whole Reformation, which could never have been compassed, if private men have not a right to judge for themselves; on the contrary they think every man is bound to judge for himself, which indeed he ought to do, in the fear of GOD, and with all humility and caution. They look on all these notions as steps towards popery though they do not conclude, that all those who have made them, designed that by so doing.

This is a short account of the *Low Church-men's* notions, with rela-tion to matters of religion among us: as to our temporal concerns, they think all that obedience and submission that is settled by our laws, to the persons of our Princes, ought to be paid them for conscience sake: but if a misguided Prince shall take on him to dissolve our Constitu-tion, and to subject the laws to his pleasure, they think that if God offers a remedy, it is to be received with all thankfulness. For these reasons they rejoiced in the Revolution, and continue faithful and true to the settlement then made; and to the subsequent settlements. They think there is a full power in the legislature to settle the Crown, and to secure the nations: and so they have taken the oaths enjoined with a good conscience, and with fixed resolutions of adhering firmly to them, without any other views but such as the laws and oaths pur-suant to them do direct. They know of no unalterable or indefeasible right, but what is founded on the law.

This is their fixed principle; and they are the more fixed in this, when they remember that a Prince educated among us, and singularly obliged by the zeal our Church expressed for his advancement to the throne, upon which he made great acknowledgments and promises, and who by his temper seemed as much inclined to keep them as his religion could admit of; yet upon his elevation did so entirely forget all this, that he seemed peculiarly sharpened against those, who, of all others, had the least reason to have expected it from him.

This was notorious and evident in the father: what then can be expected from him who calls himself his son, who has had his breed-ing in an absolute government where Protestants are persecuted with an unrelenting cruelty, and who has been obliged to wander so long beyond sea, and stands attained and abjured here, and is loaded with other indignities, but that as his religion is still the same cruel and bloody conspiracy against Protestants that it was, so it must have its full swing in one sharpened by so much provocation.

It betrays a monstrous ignorance of the principles and maxims, as well as of the history of popery, to imagine that they can ever depart from the design of extirpating heretics settled by so much authority, held sacred by them. Every look into the *Low Church-man* towards a *popish* Pretender, is to him both perjury and treason.

I have thus freely opened all that I know of the principles of those called the *Low Church-men* among us. I will not pretend to tell what are the principles of those called *High Church-men;* I know them too little to pretend to tell what their maxims and views are. I will with great joy own my mistakes and misapprehensions of any of them who upon this candid avowing what the *Low Church-men* hold, will come to have more just and more charitable thoughts of them, and upon that will concur with them in such measures and counsels as may yet give us some hope, if that is not now too late, or may be at least an abatement of our misery, if not a reprieve from it. I unwillingly mention a long disappointment among us as to Convocation[52] matters.

I will avoid saying anything that may give new irritation, my design being to do all I can to heal our breaches. I will not enter into the merits of the cause further, than to observe that the bishops have begun no new practices, but go in the steps in which their predecessors went, without varying from their practice in a title. They find themselves bound down to the methods they adhere to by such a series of precedents, that unless the legislature interposes, they think they cannot alter them. They have made no new attempts, nor have they invaded any rights of which they found the clergy in possession. And what is there in all this to occasion such tragical outcries? And to engage so many of the bodies of the clergy into jealousies of their bishops, and into combinations against them, as if they were betraying the Church and its liberties.

---

[52]Convocation (specifically, the Convocation of Canterbury) was the ancient provincial assembly of the representatives of the English clergy. In the late seventeenth and early eighteenth centuries, convocation served as the site of much acrimony between high and low church clerics—the intensity of which led to the effective suspension of the institution for more than a century.

32

JAMES II

Declaration of Indulgence

April 4, 1687

Frustrated by the refusal of his Tory allies to repeal the laws that had prevented Roman Catholics (and Protestant Nonconformists) from worshiping freely and serving in political or military offices, James II chose to sidestep Parliament by issuing a declaration that rendered the parliamentary statutes toothless. In contemporary legal parlance, he dispensed with the laws. This declaration was almost certainly written on the monarch's behalf by William Penn. It is interesting to note the limitations placed on religious practices insisted upon in the declaration: religious services that promoted political criticism and private religious services were explicitly forbidden.

It having pleased Almighty God not only to bring us to the imperial crown of these kingdoms through the greatest difficulties, but to preserve us by a more than ordinary providence upon the throne of our royal ancestors, there is nothing now that we so earnestly desire, as to establish our government on such a foundation as may make our subjects happy, and unite them to us by inclination as well as duty; which we think can be done by no means so effectually as by granting to them the free exercise of their religion for the time to come, and add that to the perfect enjoyment of their property, which has never been in any case invaded by us since our coming to the crown which, being the two things men value most, shall ever be preserved in these kingdoms during our reign over them as the truest methods of their peace and our glory.

We cannot but heartily wish, as it will easily be believed, that all the people of our dominions were members of the Catholic Church, yet we humbly thank Almighty God it is and has of long time been our constant sense and opinion (which upon diverse occasions we have

His Majesties Gracious Declaration to All His Loving Subjects for Liberty of Conscience (London: [April 4,] 1687).

declared) that conscience ought not to be constrained, nor people forced in matters of mere religion. It has ever been directly contrary to our inclination, as we think it is to the interest of government, which it destroys by spoiling trade, depopulating countries, and discouraging strangers, and finally, that it never obtained the end for which it was employed, and in this we are the more confirmed by the reflections we have made upon the conduct of the four last reigns. For after all the frequent and pressing endeavors that were used in each of them, to reduce this kingdom to an exact conformity in religion, it is visible the success has not answered the design, and that the difficulty is invincible. We therefore out of our princely care and affection unto all our loving subjects, that they may live at ease and quiet and for the increase of trade and encouragement of strangers, have thought fit by virtue of our royal prerogative to issue forth this our declaration of indulgence, making no doubt of the concurrence of our two houses of Parliament, when we shall think it convenient for them to meet.

In the first place we do declare that we will protect and maintain our archbishops, bishops, and clergy and all other our subjects of the Church of England, in the free exercise of their religion, as by law established and in the quiet and full enjoyment of all their possessions without any molestation or disturbance whatsoever.

We do likewise declare that it is our royal will and pleasure that from henceforth the execution of all and all manner of penal laws in matters ecclesiastical, for not coming to church, or not receiving the sacrament or for any other nonconformity to the religion established, or for or by reason of the exercise of religion in any manner whatsoever be immediately suspended; and the further execution of the said penal laws and every of them is hereby suspended.

And to the end that by the liberty hereby granted the peace and security of our government in the practice thereof may not be endangered, we have thought fit, and do hereby straightly charge and command all our loving subjects that, as we do freely give them leave to meet and serve God after their own way and manner, be it in private houses or places purposely hired and built for that use, so that they take especial care, that nothing be preached or taught amongst them which may any ways tend to alienate the hearts of our people from us or our government; and that their meetings and assemblies be peaceably, openly, and publicly held, and all persons freely admitted to them; and that they do signify and make known to some one or more of the next justices of the peace what place or places they set apart for those uses.

And that all our subjects may enjoy such their religions assemblies with greater assurance and protection we have thought it requisite and do hereby command that no disturbance of any kind be made or given unto them, under pain of our displeasure and to be further proceeded against with the uttermost severity.

And forasmuch as we are desirous to have the benefit of the service of all our loving subjects which by the law of nature is inseparably annexed to, and inherent in our royal person, and that none of our subjects may for the future be under any discouragement or disability (who are otherwise well inclined and fit to serve us) by reason of some oaths or tests that have been usually administered on such occasions: we do hereby declare that it is our royal will and pleasure that the oaths commonly called the Oaths of Supremacy and Allegiance, and also the several Tests and declarations mentioned in the acts of Parliament made in the 25th and 30th years of the reign of our late royal brother King Charles the Second shall not at any time hereafter be required to be taken, declared, or subscribed by any person or persons whatsoever, who is or shall be employed in any office or place of trust either civil or military under us or in our government. And we do further declare it to be our pleasure and intention from time to time hereafter to grant our royal dispensations under our great seal to all our loving subjects so to be employed who shall not take the said oaths or subscribe or declare the said tests or declarations in the above mentioned acts and every of them.

And to the end that all our loving subjects may receive and enjoy the full benefit and advantage of our gracious indulgence hereby intended, and may be acquitted and discharged from all pains, penalties, forfeitures, and disabilities by them or any of them incurred or forfeited, on which they shall or may at any time hereafter be liable to, for or by reason of their nonconformity, or the exercise of their religion, and from all suits, troubles, or disturbances for the same: we do hereby give our free and ample pardon unto all nonconformists, recusants, and other our loving subjects, for all crimes and things by them committed or done contrary to the penal laws formerly made relating to religion and the profession or exercise thereof, hereby declaring that this, our royal pardon and indemnity, shall be as good and effectual to all intents and purposes as if every individual person had been therein particularly named, or had particular pardons under our great seal, which we do likewise declare shall from time to time be granted unto any person or persons desiring the same: willing and requiring our judges, justices, and other officers to take notice of and obey our royal will and pleasure herein before declared.

And although the freedom and assurance we have hereby given in relation to religion and property might be sufficient to remove from the minds of our loving subjects all fears and jealousies in relation to either, yet we have thought fit further to declare that we will maintain them in all their properties and possessions, as well of church and abbey lands, as in any other their lands and properties whatsoever.

33

JAMES JOHNSTON

Letters regarding Nonconformist Opinion

1687

James Johnston (1655–1737) was a Scottish Presbyterian lawyer and a cousin of Gilbert Burnet. His family had fled into exile in 1663 when his father, Archibald, Lord Warriston, was executed for treason. In the 1680s, he was closely associated with William III's court in the Dutch Republic. After the revolution, he was immediately employed in sensitive diplomatic posts. In these letters, he describes the surprising turn in Nonconformist opinion in late 1687. After fierce persecution between 1683 and 1685, England's Nonconformist community welcomed James II's declaration as a miraculous intervention. However, in the high-level secret communications excerpted here, Johnston suggested that Nonconformists quickly lost their enthusiasm for James's policies.

[To Willem Bentinck, November 17, 1687]

The Presbyterians and Independents are coming off from the fondness they had at first for the toleration, and the court begins to suspect it. It is evident [that the Nonconformists] only juggle, for in many places, to my certain knowledge, such of them as declare themselves for taking off of the Test etc. have promised their voices to men who have told them they will never consent to it.

James Johnston to Willem Bentinck, November 17, 1687, Nottingham University Library, MSS PwA 2099b; James Johnston to ?, December 21, 1687, Nottingham University Library, MSS PwA 2120b.

[To Unknown Recipient, December 21, 1687]

They begin to believe at court that the present sheriffs will not do the business they were made for, and what they have done in the corporations hitherto will never have the expected effect for they have no reason to think themselves sure of the Dissenters they have put in. The business of Magdalen College[53] has lost them a great many of the Dissenters.

[53] James II attempted to install a Roman Catholic president at Magdalen College, Oxford (1687–88), against the protests of the fellows, all but two of whom were eventually suspended for their refusal to accede to the king's wishes.

34

ROGER MORRICE

A Londoner's View of Nonconformist Sentiment

October 29, 1687

Roger Morrice was a politically well-connected London Presbyterian cleric. He had informants at court, and he kept his ear to the ground in London. His diary provides a remarkably rich account of late-seventeenth-century political, religious, and social life from the perspective of a Nonconformist Londoner. This passage describes Nonconformist attitudes.

[A prominent Dissenter told James II that] there were some Independents, Anabaptists, and Quakers that would do all [the government wished], but they were extraordinary few comparatively to the Presbyterians, in whom the strength of the Dissenters in England lay, and they could do no more than let others have free exercise of their religion. Neither could the crown expect it [support of the repeal of

Roger Morrice, "Ent'ring Book," October 29, 1687, Doctor Williams' Library, MSS 31Q, 181.

the Test Acts] from them, for they did not need such an indulgence themselves for they could go to church and so were not in danger of falling under the fury of the churchmen [clergy and laity of the Church of England] because their own principles would allow them to avoid it, and they rather desired a good understanding with the sober churchmen.

35

Catholic Attitudes toward the Religious Policies of James II
January 12, 1688

While James II, himself a convert to Catholicism, pursued religious policies that were very popular among recent converts, older Catholic families did not necessarily share his views. Controversy arose over Dutch Grand Pensionary Gaspar Fagel's widely circulated letter, which criticized James II's religious policies and authoritatively committed William and Mary to the cause of religious toleration, while reassuring Anglicans that the Test Act would not be repealed. This letter and the controversy that ensued provided an anonymous pamphleteer an opportunity to reflect on divisions within England's Catholic community.

I know Roman Catholics that . . . see the great difficulty of getting the Test repealed, and withal they doubt whether it is their interest that it should be repealed or not. They fear needy, violent men might get into employments [in the government] who would put His Majesty on doing things that might ruin them and their posterity. They are certainly in the right of it.

Reflexions on Monsieur Fagel's Letter, January 12, 1688, 3.

36

JAMES WELLWOOD

Treatment of Catholics after the Revolution

July 3, 1689

*Many Catholics feared that in the wake of widespread anti-Catholic vio-
lence in November and December 1688, the postrevolution regime would
be compelled to initiate a new wave of religious persecution. In the
middle of 1689, Whig James Wellwood (1652–1727), no doubt with an
eye on William III's continental Roman Catholic allies, sought to allay
Catholic fears in this piece from the newspaper* Mercurius Reformatus.

Now when we are in a great measure delivered from that ruin, [the
Roman Catholics] were hastening upon us; and when it is in the power
of our hands to retaliate all their injuries upon their own heads, there
is not one drop of Roman Catholic blood spilt in both these nations,
either on the scaffold or in the field; there is not any of their estates
sequestered, nor the just penalties they have incurred by act of Parliament, exacted. Not only is it thus, but His Majesty has again and again
recommended to his Parliament an act of indemnity to put them out of
a possibility of being called into question for their former miscarriages, and the Parliament itself goes on in it with the greatest application possible. I find the Roman Catholics of England have all the
reason in the world to admire the goodness of our king, the generosity of the Parliament, and the kindness of the people in allowing them
so fair quarters, after they have deserved so ill at their hands. To conclude this period, the Roman Catholics may know what to expect from
his present Majesty, by that expression of his worth to be engraved in
durable brass to future ages, when at his acceptation of the crown of
Scotland, and taking the coronation oath of that kingdom to root out
heretics, he was pleased to express himself in these golden words, "I
do not mean by these words, to be under any necessity to become a
persecutor," and did thereupon require the Scotch commissioners, as
witnesses, that he had signified so much in taking his oath.

James Wellwood, *Mercurius Reformatus*, July 3, 1689, 2.

Roger L'Estrange and John Locke as Case Study

The late seventeenth century was, as several commentators have observed, an age of scribblers. By this they meant that there was a mass of readily available political and religious commentary. Most of these works were ephemeral. However, the political and religious works of John Locke have had a remarkable staying power. They are now routinely assigned in undergraduate and secondary school surveys of the history of ideas and the history of political thought. This section seeks to set some of Locke's writings against those of one of his chief contemporary antagonists, Roger L'Estrange. Locke was a great defender of the postrevolutionary regime, while L'Estrange had been one of the chief government apologists under Charles II and James II.

37

ROGER L'ESTRANGE

The Case for Royal Power

1681–1683

Sir Roger L'Estrange (1616–1704) was the most prolific and most successful journalist in the late seventeenth century. Not only did he write newsletters, newspapers, and pamphlets defending the policies of Charles II and James II, he also served as surveyor of the press. L'Estrange relentlessly hunted down and closed illegal presses that were publishing antigovernment propaganda. One of his most successful publishing exercises was his newspaper, the Observator in Dialogue. *This paper always discussed the hot topics of the day in dialogue form, with the defenders of the Whig or Trimmer (moderate) positions being invariably pilloried by*

Roger L'Estrange, *Observator in Dialogue*, no. 1, April 13, 1681; no. 50, September 7, 1681; no. 157, June 19, 1682; no. 169, July 12, 1682; no. 241, November 15, 1682; no. 287, February 10, 1683; no. 387, August 15, 1683.

the proponent of Tory views. It is worth contrasting the arguments against religious Nonconformity advanced by L'Estrange and by the high church- man George Hickes (see Document 30).

[April 13, 1681]

Take it in few words then. My business is to encounter the faction, and to vindicate the government; to detect their forgeries; to lay open the rankness of their calumnies and malice; to refute their seditious doctrines; to expose their hypocrisy, and the bloody design that is car- ried on, under the name and semblance of religion; and, in short, to lift up the cloak of the true Protestant (as he christens himself) and to show the people the Jesuit that lies skulking under it.

[September 7, 1681]

Tory. . . . And I call it sedition, to publish false and scandalous rumors against the government, and to posses the people with groundless jealousies of their superiors. I call it sedition, to arraign the King's pro- ceedings; to revile him for his declarations; to expostulate his just pre- rogatives; and under the notion of apprehending the danger of arbitrary power, to expose his sacred majesty for a tyrant; and who at last so fearful of this inundation of absolute power as the scum of the multitude; a sort of people, of servile souls, and conditions, that have nothing to lose, nor, in truth, any thing to hope for, but from the ruins of a common confusion. . . . I call it a seditious doctrine, the denial of the King's supremacy; and ranging an imperial prince in a state of co- ordination with his subjects. And I call it a seditious maxim too, that subjects may, in any case, take up arms against their sovereign. I reckon upon it as very near bordering upon treason, for subjects to alienate their allegiance, from their lawful prince, and to transfer it to any body of men whatsoever: By offering them the service, of their lives and fortunes, without any reserve whatsoever; and even against the King himself, if that should come to be the question. . . .

[June 19, 1682]

Whig. But will you defend the Protestant Religion with your lives and fortunes under a popish successor?

Tory. And I say again: how will you destroy a popish successor, and yet call yourselves Protestants? When in so doing, you act contrary to the principles, and doctrine of your profession? But pray you mark it well; and you'll find, that as we have no right to invade his legal title; (so taking it as worst) neither has he any power to take away our religion, for it is not a thing liable to a capture. A man's body may be imprisoned, shot, mangled, burnt, and his goods seized; but his conscience stands impregnable. How ridiculous were it now to urge a contending by force for the preserving of that which cannot be taken away by force; when it is yet adjudged a rebellion to take up arms against the King and the laws, in the defense of our liberties and possessions, which may be taken away by force?

Whig. The laws of a man's country are the measures of all civil obedience.

Tory. . . . and the rule holds as well for the duty of passive obedience, how Mohammedan and Turkish soever he is pleased to make it. Unless he can produce some exception in law, in the case of religion to the general interdiction of peoples taking up arms, without the authority and commission of their sovereign. If you would but lay aside the partiality and prejudice you bring to all discourses of this quality, I should lay this consideration before you. The law of succession is clear as the sun; and the laws against Dissenters are as clear as that: so that you have manifestly the law against you both ways. You are afraid of losing that which cannot be taken away; and upon that fantastical apprehension, the course of the government itself must be dissolved to gratify your pretended scruples. Why should not the King now, that has the law and all the reason in the world on his side, pass this reflection upon the Dissenters? The law pronounces these people to be dangerous to the monarchy: they have never suffered any government to be quiet since they came into the world: they teased Queen Elizabeth almost out of her life; persecuted and galled the very soul of King James [I]; destroyed the late king; the monarchy; the Church; the order of it; and all those that asserted the cause of their sovereign and their religion; there was no popish successor then suggested; but the bare outcries of a popish king did the work, though he signed the contrary with his blood. These men, while they make a noise where there is no danger, they carry on a more dangerous design, without noise. What can be more expedient now (I might have said necessary), then for the government to secure itself against these people according to law, that are so pragmatical to embroil and confound it against law?

[July 12, 1682]

Whig. Where's the harm, or danger to the government of letting men worship according to their consciences?

Tory. Prithee why should not the King govern according to his conscience, as well as the subject worship according to theirs; Especially where his conscience is according to the law, and theirs, against it. (Beside the certainty of error in so many divided opinions.) And then how comes it at the same time to be Tyranny, to pass the bounds of the laws, and yet persecution to command them to be executed?

Whig. You speak as if the easing of Dissenters and the securing of the government were inconsistent.

Tory. I do so: And that it is impossible for either the King or the Church to be safe under that license which you call an easing of Dissenters: for what is it but an allowance of a complication of schism and sedition in the utmost extent? For it terminates in an allowance of practice, as well as of profession; and there is nothing so enormous but it may put on the cloak of conscience to cover it. Conscientious rapine, conscientious sacrilege, blood, perjury, rebellion, regicide: carry your eye, in short, through all the steps of villainy and wickedness, from the murder of Strafford[54] to the scaffold of the late king; and from thence through all the mazes of blasphemy, slavery and oppression to the very restoration of his sacred majesty; and you'd find the devil's motto to be conscience; and conscience still; seeking the Lord only where he was not to be found; and through all the by-ways that lead to the very gates of hell. Prithee tell me, were you ever? Will you ever be satisfied? Or is it possible that ever you should be so; but in the destruction of those from whom you pretend to ask relief? Do you not damn one another, and cut throats among yourselves, upon principles absolutely irreconcilable? And what is it then that you pray for, but under the notional sham of an indulgence; the liberty of turning three kingdoms once again into a shambles; first by uniting your arms against the King, the Church and the laws; and then to fight it over again among yourselves for the booty.

Whig. How does this fierceness against the whole body of Dissenters stand with your former acknowledgments and confessions that

---

[54]Thomas Wentworth, 1st Earl of Strafford (1593–1641), was appointed lord deputy of Ireland in 1632 by Charles I. His management of Charles I's affairs in the aftermath of the disastrous Bishops' Wars earned him the hostility of the Commons. He was impeached in November 1640 and tried the following spring; he was executed on May 10, 1641.

nine parts of them at least of ten, are a well-meaning; and only a deluded sort of people?

Tory. Prithee I say so still: but they have crafty and designing snaps in the head of them; and their well-meaning errors are yet more pernicious to the state then the most rancorous malice; for the honesty of the intention gives a reputation to the delusion. Would you be tolerated with a respect to your consciences? Turks and pagans, in that latitude, have as good a title to indulgence as you have.

[November 15, 1682]

Trimmer. Is it not a Christian office to endeavor a fair understanding betwixt party and party; and to bring differences and disputes into a state of accommodation?

Observator. Yes, it is so; provided you make it your business to procure an agreement in the right, not in the wrong; and in the truth, and reason of the matter; not in a conspiracy, or faction; for otherwise the more united, the worse; when that union comes to terminate in a confederacy, or mistake.

[February 10, 1683]

Trimmer. 'Tis understood of the English nation.

Observator. That's the expounding one riddle by another. The people are the nation; and the nation is the people: but do ye speak of the multitude, or of the community? If of the community, why do ye not rather call it the government? If of the multitude; they have no right of acting, judging, or interposing otherwise then in obedience and submission to the rules of order and society. So that your telling of people that they may do this or that; is the same thing with telling them, that if they don't like their laws and their governors, they may provide better, and shift for themselves: now here's a sedition, not only licensed, but encouraged: for being couched in this trimming, middling way; it speaks plain English to the rabble; though the law will scarce lay hold on it. 'Tis the very *Veni, Vidi, Vici* of the cause; first, that the people are the source of power. Secondly, that upon maladministration they may recall their power. And thirdly, to tell 'em, gentlemen, you are most damnably abused, up and be doing. To pass over your engrossing the intent of people and nation, to yourselves; as if all the royalists and conformists were no more than vagabonds and outlaws.

[August 15, 1683]

Observator. Why, I do tell you over and over, that a civil monarchy may as well subsist with a hundred and fifty independent commonwealths in the belly of it, as an ecclesiastical monarchy, with so many independent and republican schisms in it. Their interest and their principles can never stand together; and in this case, it holds both ways; and not only, "No Bishop, No King," but "No King, No Bishop" too. Where there is a war declared in the very heart of a constitution, or of any sort of people, against the public polity and order of the state; there wants nothing but a fair opportunity for putting those dispositions into act, by an open rupture: so that the prince that suffers a growing and spreading schism in his dominions is to make account that he entertains an enemy army within his bowels upon free quarter; that's ready to march, at any time, upon four and twenty hours warning. The Presbyterian congregations; the Independent, the Anabaptist, the Millenary, &c. are nothing in the world, but the blue, the red, and green, the yellow regiments: And these are not distinctions of persuasion, but of faction: and the whole body of them makes up the church militant according to the letter.

Trimmer. So that upon your proposition, it is not possible for a Dissenter to be an honest man. Prithee suppose a false religion were uppermost; must every man be made a criminal of state, that will not go along with it?

Observator. I will allow, that a man may dissent, and yet be honest; that the public may be in the wrong, and a private man in the right: but that dissent must be kept within the compass then: nay, and the very truth must be managed with a respect to the civil peace. Our Savior himself both preached, and practiced submission, even to a pagan emperor, and the giving of Caesar his due and yet the Son of Man did not forbear resistance, upon our apostate's argument, that the emperor would have been too hard for him. There may be matter of conscience in a single dissent; but the gathering of churches and making of parties upon it, is most intolerable and impious; and therefore the law has, with great reason, defined all separate assemblies, (notwithstanding their pretences of religious worship) to be seditious meetings. And they are so in their original intent, as well as we have found them so, in issue and effect. Where any man speaks for more than himself, and that they come to stickle, one man for another, there's a manifest agreement upon mischief: and it is not longer conscience, but riot and clamor: but when one sect comes to plead for all the rest;

and every several sect, for the whole schism; under the mysterious notion of true Protestant Dissenters, this is a palpable confederacy; without the least shadow of religion to countenance it: unless you can reconcile truth to itself, under so many various forms; and such killing and unsociable contradiction.

38

ROGER L'ESTRANGE

The Economics of Fisheries

1674

Though economic historians tell us that fisheries were not terribly signifi-cant economically in the later seventeenth century, they loomed large in economic debates. Fisheries were understood to be a kind of marine agri-cultural project. They consisted of harvesting a large but finite resource in what many understood to be sovereign territory. Fishery companies were invariably royalist and then Tory projects. Unsurprisingly, then, L'Estrange's most sustained discussion of his economic ideas came in this pamphlet advocating a national fishery company. It is worth noting that the Dutch provided England's main economic competition, just as they did in the East Indies.

1. The Fishery is of great, and certain advantage.

Touching the advantages of the fishery [of England], I presume there will be no dispute, since it is granted on all hands, that the Dutch are beholding to it for the rise, and support of their greatness; for their reputation abroad, and for their strength at home: insomuch that the herring, cod, and ling taken in his Majesty's seas, by the Dutch, and other strangers, are valued . . . at no less than ten millions of pounds sterling [per annum]; which computation has been often published, and constantly received for current, without contradiction.

Roger L'Estrange, *A Discourse of the Fishery* (London: printed for Henry Brome, 1674), 1–3, 9–10.

2. The fishery lies fairer for the subjects of his Majesty of Great Britain, than for the Hollanders.

As the fishery is very considerable, so it lies much fairer for us, than for them, in regard that we have many advantages toward it, which the Dutch want, and that we hardly want any thing which they have; save only industry, which may be easily promoted by good order, and discipline.

First, we have the fish upon our coasts, (I might have said upon our shores) where in case of storm, unlading, taking in provisions, or the like; it is seldom above 4 or 5 hours work (and most commonly not so much) to recover a harbor, and without any loss of time, to refit, and put to sea again; whereas the Dutch have usually some 200 leagues to sail before they come to their fishing; and there they lie at the mercy of the winds, for want of a port to friend: and in case of unlading, they have as far back again; which takes up a great deal of time, hinders their business, and endangers the loss of their Markets. It is true, that they have their yagers[55] many times, to take off their fish at sea, and refurnish them with cask, and other necessaries; but if it happens to be a rolling sea, they must lie still, and wait for a calm; whereas with us that are in harbor, the work of unlading, repacking, and sending our fish away to the first market, goes on in all weathers. So that in respect of the nearness of the fishing, we have much the better of them: and no less, in the commodiousness of our ports and creeks to receive the buses upon all occasions. . . .

It would be endless to run through all the particulars; how it begets commerce; fills his Majesty's coffers; peoples his dominions; and consequently raises the price of land; enriches the merchant, both by exportation, and importation; and the tradesman, by setting all hands to work: for it is remarkable, that 10,000 £. adventure in the fishery, employs more people, than 50,000 £. in any other trade whatsoever, clothing excepted. It excites industry, and clears us of loiterers, and beggars. Insomuch, that ordinary servants make themselves fortunes, by working of nets, at spare hours, and adventuring them in the fishery. . . .

If we let our Navigation fall, we are Lost; and how to support, and supply it, without the Fishery, I do not Comprehend; The Man of War, and the Merchant-man, consume Seamen, and Breed none. The Collier[56] brings up, now and then an Apprentice, but still spends more

---

[55] Workers.
[56] A ship carrying coal.

than he makes. The only (and the Common) Nursery of Seamen is the Fishery; where every Busse[57] bring up (it may be) 6, 8, or 10 new men every Year; so that our Fishery is just as Necessary to our Navigation, as our Navigation is to our safety, and well-being. And it is well enough observed, that All Princes and States, are stronger or Weaker, at Sea, according to the Measures of their Fishery. . . .

As we can do nothing at sea without the fishery, so I am afraid we shall make as ill shift at land, for we have a bold coast, and for want of people upon it, to defend it, we lie open to a thousand mischiefs. The fishery will relieve us in this too; by planting a trade there, which will draw on commerce, and consequently repeople and strengthen us. If it be asked me, how we have done for seamen all this while? I answer, that we have done for seamen, as some people do for money; that have but a thousand pound in the world, and play away five hundred of it in a night: we spend upon the main stock, and it will never hold out. It has been our fishery (even poor as it is) that has supported us all this while, and when that dies, a man may foretell without the help of an oracle, that the glory of England will not long outlive it.

[57] Fishing ship usually used for herring fishing.

39

JOHN LOCKE

A Defense of Toleration

1689

John Locke (1632–1704) served throughout the 1670s as secretary and adviser to the earl of Shaftesbury, the Whig political leader. He fled to Holland in 1683, where he conversed extensively with a circle of Dutch and French Huguenot advocates of religious toleration. This letter was originally written to Philip Van Limborch, one of the members of this circle, in Latin. It was translated into English by William Popple, another noted political radical. Locke returned to England in February 1689 and was immediately offered a diplomatic post, which he declined.

John Locke, *A Letter concerning Toleration* (London, 1689), 1–13, 21–27, 40–42, 45–57.

In 1689, he published both A Letter concerning Toleration *and the* Two Treatises of Government.

Honored Sir,

Since you are pleased to inquire what are my thoughts about the mutual toleration of Christians in their different professions of religion, I must needs answer you freely, that I esteem that toleration to be the chief characteristical mark of the true church. For whatsoever some people boast of the antiquity of places and names, or of the pomp of their outward worship; others, of the reformation of their discipline; all, of the orthodoxy of their faith; (for every one is orthodox to himself): these things, and all others of this nature, are much rather marks of men striving for power and empire over one another, than of the church of Christ. Let any one have never so true a claim to all these things, yet if he be destitute of charity, meekness, and good-will in general towards all mankind, even to those that are not Christians, he is certainly yet short of being a true Christian himself. The kings of the gentiles exercise lordship over them, said our savior to his disciples, but ye shall not be so. The business of true religion is quite another thing. It is not instituted in order to the erecting of an external pomp, nor to the obtaining of ecclesiastical dominion, nor to the exercising of compulsive force; but to the regulating of men's lives according to the rules of virtue and piety. Whosoever will lift himself under the banner of Christ, must in the first place, and above all things, make war upon his own lusts and vices. It is in vain for any man to usurp the name of Christian, without holiness of life, purity of manners, and benignity and meekness of spirit. . . .

That any man should think fit to cause another man, whose salvation he heartily desires, to expire in torments, and that even in an unconverted estate, would, I confess, seem very strange to me, and, I think, to any other also. But no body, surely, will ever believe that such a carriage can proceed from charity, love, or good will. If any one maintain that men ought to be compelled by fire and sword to profess certain doctrines, and conform to this or that exterior worship, without any regard had unto their morals; if any one endeavor to convert those that are erroneous unto the faith, by forcing them to profess things that they do not believe, and allowing them to practice things that the Gospel does not permit; it cannot be doubted indeed but such a one is desirous to have a numerous assembly joined in the same profession with himself; but that he principally intends by those means to compose a truly Christian church, is altogether incredible. . . . Though if infidels were to be converted by force, if those that are either blind or obstinate were to be drawn off from their errors by armed soldiers, we know very well that it was much more easy for him to do it with armies of heavenly legions, than for any son of the church, how potent soever, with all his dragoons.

. . . That some may not color their spirit of persecution and unchristian cruelty with a pretence of care of the public weal, and observation of the laws; and that others, under pretence of religion, may not seek impunity for their libertinism and licentiousness; in a word, that none may impose either upon himself or others, by the pretences of loyalty and obedience to the prince, or of tenderness and sincerity in the worship of God; I esteem it above all things necessarily to distinguish exactly the business of civil government from that of religion, and to settle the just bounds that lie between the one and the other. If this be not done, there can be no end put to the controversies that will be always arising, between those that have, or at least pretend to have, on the one side, a concernment for the interest of men's souls, and on the other side, a care of the commonwealth. . . .

Now that the whole jurisdiction of the magistrate reaches only to these civil concernments; and that all civil power, right and dominion, is bounded and confined to the only care of promoting these things; and that it neither can nor ought in any manner to be extended to the salvation of souls, these following considerations seem unto me abundantly to demonstrate.

First, because the care of souls is not committed to the civil magistrate any more than to other men. It is not committed unto him, I say, by God; because it appears not that God has ever given any such authority to one man over another as to compel any one to his religion. Nor can any such power be vested in the magistrate by the consent of the people; because no man can so far abandon the care of his own salvation, as blindly to leave it to the choice of any other, whether prince or subject, to prescribe to him what faith or worship he shall embrace. For no man can, if he would, conform his faith to the dictates of another. All the life and power of true religion consists in the inward and full persuasion of the mind; and faith is not faith without believing. Whatever profession we make, to whatever outward worship we conform, if we are not fully satisfied in our own mind that the one is true, and the other well pleasing unto God, such profession and such practice, far from being any furtherance, are indeed great obstacles to our salvation. For in this manner, instead of expiating other sins by the exercise of religion, I say in offering thus unto God Almighty such a worship as we esteem to be displeasing unto him, we add unto the number of our other sins, those also of hypocrisy, and contempt of his divine majesty.

In the second place, the care of souls cannot belong to the civil magistrate, because his power consists only in outward force; but true and saving religion consists in the inward persuasion of the mind, without which nothing can be acceptable to God. And such is the nature of the understanding, that it cannot be compelled to the belief of any thing by outward force. Confiscation of estate, imprisonment, torments, nothing of that nature can have any such efficacy as to make men change the inward judgment that they have framed of things.

In the third place, the care of the salvation of men's souls cannot belong to the magistrate; because, though the rigor of laws and the force of penalties were capable to convince and change men's minds, yet would not that help at all to the salvation of their souls. For there being but one truth, one way to heaven; what hopes is there that more men would be led into it, if they had no rules but the religion of the court, and were put under a necessity to quit the light of their own reason, and oppose the dictates of their own consciences, and blindly to resign up themselves to the will of their governors, and to the religion, which either ignorance, ambition, or superstition had chanced to establish in the countries where they were born? In the variety and contradiction of opinions in religion, wherein the princes of the world are as much divided as in their Secular interests, the narrow way would be much straitened; one country alone would be in the right, and all the rest of the world put under an obligation of following their princes in the ways that lead to destruction; and that which heightens the absurdity, and very ill suits the notion of a deity, men would owe their eternal happiness or misery to the places of their nativity. . . .

Let us now consider what a church is. A church then I take to be a voluntary society of men, joining themselves together of their own accord, in order to the public worshipping of God in such a manner as they judge acceptable to him, and effectual to the salvation of their souls. I say it is a free and voluntary society. No body is born a member of any church; otherwise the religion of parents would descend unto children, by the same right of inheritance as their temporal estates, and every one would hold his faith by the same tenure he does his lands; than which nothing can be imagined more absurd. Thus therefore that matter stands. No man by nature is bound unto any particular church or sect, but every one joins himself voluntarily to that society in which he believes he has found that profession and worship which is truly acceptable to God. The hopes of salvation, as it was the only cause of his entrance into that communion, so it can be the only reason of his stay there. For if afterwards he discovers any thing either erroneous in the doctrine, or incongruous in the worship of that society to which he has joined himself, why should it not be as free for him to go out as it was to enter? No member of a religious society can be tied with any other bonds but what proceed from the certain expectation of eternal life. A church then is a society of members voluntarily uniting to this end.

It follows now that we consider what is the power of this church, and unto what laws it is subject.

Forasmuch as no society, how free soever, or upon whatsoever slight occasion instituted, (whether of philosophers for learning, of merchants for commerce, or of men of leisure for mutual conversation and discourse), no church or company, I say, can in the least subsist and hold together, but will presently dissolve and break to pieces, unless it be regulated by some laws, and the members all consent to observe some order. Place and time of meeting must be agreed on; rules for admitting and excluding members must be established; distinction of officers, and putting things into a regular course, and such like, cannot be omitted. But since the joining together of several members into this church-society, as has already been demonstrated, is absolutely free and spontaneous, it necessarily follows, that the right of making its laws can belong to none but the society itself, or at least (which is the same thing) to those whom the society by common consent has authorized thereunto. . . .

But let us grant unto these zealots, who condemn all things that are not of their mode, that from these circumstances arise different ends. What shall we conclude from thence? There is only one of these which is the true way to eternal happiness. But in this great variety of ways that men follow, it is still doubted which is this right one. Now neither the care of the commonwealth, nor the right of enacting laws, does discover this way that leads to heaven more certainly to the magistrate, than every private man's search and study discovers it unto himself. I have a weak body, sunk under a languishing disease, for which (I suppose) there is one only remedy, but that unknown. Does it therefore belong unto the magistrate to prescribe me a remedy, because there is but one, and because it is unknown? Because there is but one way for me to escape death, will it therefore be safe for me to do whatsoever the magistrate ordains? Those things that every man ought sincerely to enquire unto himself, and by meditation, study, search, and his own endeavors, attain the knowledge of, cannot be looked upon as the peculiar body of any one sort of men. Princes indeed are born superior unto other men in power, but in nature equal. Neither the right, nor the art of ruling, does necessarily carry along with it the certain knowledge of other things; and least of all of the true religion. For if it were so, how could it come to pass that the lords of the earth should differ so vastly as they do in religious matters? But let us grant that it is probable the way to eternal life may be better known by a prince than by his subjects; or at least, that in this incertitude of things, the safest and most commodious way for private persons is to follow his dictates. You will say, what then? If he should bid you follow merchandise for your livelihood, would you decline that course for fear it should not succeed? I answer: I would turn merchant upon the prince's command, because in case I should have ill success in trade, he is abundantly able to make up my loss some other way. If it be true, as he pretends, that he desires I should thrive and grow rich, he can set me up again when unsuccessful voyages have broke me. But this is not the case, in the things that regard the life to come. If there I take a wrong course, if in that respect I am once undone, it is not in the magistrate's power to repair my loss, to ease my suffering, nor to restore me in any measure, much less entirely, to a good estate. What security can be given for the kingdom of heaven? . . .

But after all, the principal constitution, and which absolutely determines this controversy, is this: although the magistrate's opinion in religion be sound, and the way that he appoints be truly evangelical, yet if I be not thoroughly persuaded thereof in my own mind, there will be no safety for me in following it. No way whatsoever that I shall walk in, against the dictates of my conscience, will ever bring me to the mansions of the blessed. I may grow rich by an art that I take not delight in; I may be cured of some disease by remedies that I have not faith in; but I cannot be saved by a religion that I distrust, and by a worship that I abhor. It is in vain for an unbeliever to take up the outward show of another man's profession. Faith only, and inward sincerity, are the things that procure acceptance with God. . . . In a word, whatsoever may be doubtful in religion, yet this at least is certain, that no religion, which I believe not to be true, can be either true, or profitable unto me. In vain therefore do princes compel their subjects to come into their church communion, under pretence of saving their souls. If they believe, they will come of their own accord; if they believe not, their coming will nothing avail them. How great soever, in sin, may be the pretence of good-will, and charity, and concern for the salvation of men's souls, men cannot be forced to be saved whether they will or no. And therefore, when all is done, they must be left to their own consciences.

Having thus at length freed men from all dominion over one another in matters of religion, let us now consider what they are to do. All men know and acknowledge that God ought to be publicly worshipped. Why otherwise do they compel one another unto the public assemblies? Men therefore constituted in this liberty are to enter some religious society, that they may meet together, not only for mutual edification, but to own to the world that they worship God, and offer unto his divine majesty such service as they themselves are not ashamed of, and such as they think not unworthy of him; and finally, that by the purity of doctrine, holiness of life, and decent form of worship, they may draw others unto the love of the true religion, and perform such other things in religion as cannot be done by each private man apart. . . .

Further, the magistrate ought not to forbid the preaching or professing of any speculative opinions in any church, because they have no manner of relation to the civil rights of the subjects. If a Roman Catholic believe that to be really the body of Christ, which another man calls bread, he does no injury thereby to his neighbor. If a Jew does not believe the New Testament to be the word of God, he does not thereby alter any thing in men's civil rights. If a heathen doubt of both Testaments, he is not therefore to be punished as a pernicious citizen. The power of the magistrate, and the estates of the people, may be equally secure, whether any man believe these things or no. I readily grant, that these opinions are false and absurd. But the business of laws is not to provide for the truth of opinions, but for the safety and security of the commonwealth, and of every particular mans goods and person. And so it ought to be. For truth certainly would do well enough, if she were once left to shift for herself. She seldom has received, and I fear never will receive much assistance from the power of great men, to whom she is but rarely known, and more rarely welcome. She is not taught by laws, nor has she any need of force to procure her entrance into the minds of men; errors indeed prevail by the assistance of foreign and borrowed succors. But if truth makes not her way into the understanding by her own light, she will be but the weaker for any borrowed force violence can add to her. Thus much for speculative opinions. Let us now proceed to practical ones.

A good life, in which consists not the least part of religion and true piety, concerns also the civil government: and in it lies the safety both of men's souls, and of the commonwealth. Moral actions belong therefore to the jurisdiction both of the outward and inward court; both of the civil and domestic governor; I mean, both of the magistrate and conscience. Here therefore is great danger, least one of these jurisdictions entrench upon the other, and discord arise between the keeper of the public peace and the overseers of souls. But if what has been already said concerning the limits of both these governments be rightly considered, it will easily remove all difficulty in this matter.

Every man has an immortal soul, capable of eternal happiness or misery; whose happiness depending upon his believing and doing those things in this life, which are necessary to the obtaining of God's favor, and are prescribed by God to that end; it follows from thence, first, that the observance of these things is the highest obligation that lies upon mankind, and that our utmost care, application and diligence, ought to be exercised in the search and performance of them; because there is nothing in this world that is of any consideration in comparison with eternity. Secondly, that seeing one man does not violate the right of another, by his erroneous opinions, and undue manner of worship, nor is his perdition any prejudice to another man's affairs; therefore the care of each man's salvation belongs only to himself. But I would not have this understood, as if I meant hereby to condemn all charitable admonitions, and affectionate endeavors to reduce men from errors; which are indeed the greatest duty of a Christian. Any one may employ as many exhortations and arguments as he pleases, towards the promoting of another man's salvation. But all force and compulsion are to be foreborn. Nothing is to be done imperiously. No body is obliged in that matter to yield obedience unto the admonitions or injunctions of another, further than he himself is persuaded. Every man, in that, has the supreme and absolute authority at judging for himself. And the reason is, because no body else is concerned in it, nor can receive any prejudice from his conduct therein. . . .

Another more secret evil, but more dangerous to the commonwealth, is, when men arrogate to themselves, and to those of their own sect, some peculiar prerogative, covered over with a specious show of deceitful words, but in effect opposite to the civil right of the community. For example, we cannot find any sect that teaches expressly, and openly, that men are not obliged to keep their promise; that princes may be dethroned by those that differ from them in religion; or that the dominion of all things belongs only to themselves. For these things, proposed thus nakedly and plainly, would soon draw on them the eye and hand of the magistrate, and awaken all the care of the commonwealth to a watchfulness against the spreading of so dangerous an evil. But nevertheless, we find those that say the same things, in other words. What else do they mean, who teach that faith is not to be kept with heretics? Their meaning, forsooth is that the privilege of breaking faith belongs unto themselves: For they declare all that are not of their communion to be heretics, or at least may declare them so whenever they think fit. What can be the meaning of their asserting that kings excommunicated forfeit their crowns and kingdoms? It is evident that they thereby arrogate unto themselves the power of deposing kings: because they challenge the power of excommunication, as the peculiar right of their hierarchy. That dominion is founded in grace, is also an assertion by which those that maintain it do plainly lay claim to the possession of all things. For they are not so wanting to themselves as not to believe, or at least as not to profess, themselves to be the truly pious and faithful. These therefore, and the like, who attribute unto the faithful, religious and orthodox, that is, in plain terms, unto themselves, any peculiar privilege or power above other mortals, in civil governments; or who, upon pretence of religion, do challenge any manner of authority over such, as are not associated with them in their ecclesiastical communion; I say these have no right to be tolerated by the magistrate; as neither those that will not own and teach the duty of tolerating all men in matters of mere religion. For what do all these and the like doctrines signify, but that they may, and are ready upon any occasion to seize the government, and possess themselves of the estates and fortunes of their fellow-subjects; and that they only ask leave to be tolerated by the magistrate so long until they find themselves strong enough to effect it?

Again: that church can have no right to be tolerated by the magistrate, which is constituted upon such a bottom that all those who enter into it, do thereby, *ipso facto,* deliver themselves up to the protection and service of another prince. For by this means the magistrate would give way to the settling of a foreign jurisdiction in his own country, and suffer his own people to be lifted, as it were, for soldiers against his own government. . . .

Lastly, those are not at all to be tolerated who deny the being of a God. Promises, covenants, and oaths, which are the bonds of humane society, can have no hold upon an atheist. The taking away of God, though but even in thought, dissolves all. Besides also, those that by their atheism undermine and destroy all religion, can have no pretence of religion whereupon to challenge the privilege of a toleration. As for other practical opinions, though not absolutely free from all error, if they do not tend to establish domination over others, or civil impunity to the church in which they are taught, there can be no reason why they should not be tolerated. . . .

That we may draw towards a conclusion. The sum of all we drive at is, that every man may enjoy the same rights that are granted to others. Is it permitted to worship God in the Roman manner? Let it be permitted to do it in the Geneva form also. Is it permitted to speak Latin in the market-place? Let those that have a mind to it, be permitted to do it also in the church. Is it lawful for any man in his own house, to kneel, stand, sit, or use any other posture; and to clothe himself in white or black, in short or in long garments? Let it not be made unlawful to eat bread, drink wine, or wash with water, in the church. In a word: whatsoever things are left free by law in the common occasions of life, let them remain free unto every church in divine worship. Let no man's life, or body, or house, or estate, suffer any manner of prejudice upon these accounts. Can you allow of the Presbyterian discipline? Why should not the Episcopal also have what they like? Ecclesiastical authority, whether it be administered by the hands of a single person, or many, is every where the same; and neither has any jurisdiction in things civil, nor any manner of power of compulsion; nor any thing at all to do with riches and revenues, ecclesiastical assemblies, and sermons, are justified by daily experience, and public allowance. These are allowed to people of some one persuasion: why not to all? If any thing pass in a religious meeting seditiously, and contrary to the public peace, it is to be punished in the same manner, and no otherwise, than as if it had happened in a fair or market. These meetings ought not to be sanctuaries for factious and flagitious fellows: nor ought it to be less lawful for men to meet in churches than in halls: nor are one part of the subjects to be esteemed more blameable, for their meeting together, than others. Every one is to be accountable for his own actions; and no man is to be laid under a suspicion, or odium, for the fault of another. Those that are seditious, murderers, thieves, robbers, adulterers, slanderers, &c. of whatsoever church, whether national or not, ought to be punished and suppressed. But those whose doctrine is peaceable, and whose manners are pure and blameless, ought to be upon equal terms with their fellow-subjects. Thus if solemn assemblies, observations of festivals, public worship, be permitted to any one sort of professors; all these things ought to be permitted to the Presbyterians, Independents, Anabaptists, Arminians, Quakers, and others, with the same liberty. Nay, if we may openly speak the truth, and as becomes one man or another, neither pagan, nor Mahometan, nor Jew, ought to be excluded from the civil rights of the commonwealth, because of his religion. The Gospel commands no such thing. The church, which judges not those what are without, wants it not. And the commonwealth, which embraces indifferently all men that are honest, peaceable and industrious, requires it not. Shall we suffer a pagan to deal and trade with us, and shall we not suffer him to pray unto and worship God? If we allow the Jews to have private houses and dwellings amongst us, why should we not allow them to have synagogues? Is their doctrine more abominable, or is the civil peace more endangered, by their meeting in public than in their private houses? But if these things may be granted to Jews, and pagans, surely the condition of any Christians ought not to be worse than theirs in a Christian commonwealth.

40

JOHN LOCKE

Treatises on Political and Economic Arrangements

1689

John Locke's Two Treatises of Government *are justly regarded as classics of political thinking. However, they were written at a particular moment in time as an intervention in a particular political situation. Because that moment was pivotal in the creation of political and economic modernity, these texts help to illuminate the making of the modern polity. However, the force of the arguments can be lost if they are not set*

John Locke, *Two Treatises of Government* (London: printed for Awnsham Churchill, 1690), 245–46, 261–64, 345–50, 362–63, 378–82, 424–52.

in their historical context. Locke was a serious economic thinker and had served on Charles II's Council of Trade in the 1670s. In 1696, he agreed to serve on William III's Board of Trade. It is important to note that although Locke almost certainly wrote most of the Two Treatises *in the early 1680s, he only saw fit to have them printed in 1689. He clearly felt that the appropriate political moment had come. The arguments on political resistance and political economy advanced in this excerpt can thus usefully be contrasted with the claims made by Roger L'Estrange. Locke, unlike L'Estrange, argued that the people could replace a government that did not promote the good, and that property was created by human labor, not divine endowment. These were central principles of the Revolution of 1688–89.*

Chapter V. Of Property

27. Though the earth, and all inferior creatures be common to all men, yet every man has a property in his own person. This no body has any right to but himself. The labor of his body, and the work of his hands, we may say, are properly his. Whatsoever then he removed out of the state that nature has provided, and left it in, he has mixed his labor with it, and joined to it something that is his own, and thereby makes it his property. It being by him removed from the common state nature placed it in, it has by this labor something annexed to it, that excludes the common right of other men. For this labor being the unquestionable property of the laborer, no man but he can have a right to what that is once joined to, at least where there is enough, and as good left in common for others. . . .

43. An acre of land that bears here twenty bushels of wheat, and another in America, which with the same husbandry, would do the like, are, without doubt, of the same natural, intrinsic value. But yet the benefit mankind receives from one in a year is worth 5 £. and the other possibly not worth a penny; if all the profit an Indian received from it were to be valued, and sold here; at least, I may truly say, not 1/100. 'Tis labor then which puts the greatest part of value upon land, without which it would scarcely be worth any thing; 'tis to that we owe the greatest part of all its useful products; for all that the straw, bran, bread, of the acre of wheat is more worth than the product of an acre of as good land which lies waste, is all the effect of labor. For 'tis not barely the ploughman's pains, the reaper's and thresher's toil, and the baker's sweat, is to be counted into the bread we eat; the labor of

those who broke the oxen, who digged and wrought the iron and stones, who felled and framed the timber employed about the plough, mill, oven, or any other utensils, which are a vast number, requisite to this corn, from its sowing to its being made bread, must all be charged on the account of labor, and received as an effect of that: nature and the earth furnished only the almost worthless materials, as in themselves. It would be a strange catalogue of things, that industry provided and made use of, about every loaf of bread before it came to our use, if we could trace them; iron, wood, leather, bark, timber, stone, bricks, coals, lime, cloth, dying-drugs, pitch, tar, masts, ropes, and all the materials made use of in the ship, that brought any of the commodities, made use of by any of the workmen, to any part of the work, all which, it would be almost impossible, at least too long, to reckon up.

44. From all which it is evident, that though the things of nature are given in common: man (by being master of himself, and proprietor of his own person, and the actions and labor of it) had still in himself the great foundation of property: and that which made up the great part of what he applied to the support or comfort of his being, when invention and arts had improved the conveniencies of life, was perfectly his own, and did not belong in common to others.

45. Thus labor, in the beginning, gave a right of property, where ever any one was pleased to employ it, upon what was common, which remained, a long while, the far greater part, and is yet more than mankind makes use of. Men, at first, for the most part, contented themselves with what unassisted nature offered to their necessities; and though afterwards, in some parts of the world, where the increase of people and stock, with the use of money, had made land scarce, and so of some value, the several communities settled the bounds of their distinct territories, and, by laws, within themselves, regulated the properties of the private men of their society, and so, by compact and agreement, settled the property which labor and industry began. And the leagues, that have been made between several states and kingdoms, either expressly or tacitly disowning all claim and right to the land in the others' possession, have, by common consent, given up their pretences to their natural common right, which originally they had to those countries: and so have, by positive agreement, settled a property amongst themselves, in distinct parts of the world; yet there are still great tracts of ground to be found, which the inhabitants thereof, not having joined with the rest of mankind, in the consent of the use of their common money, lie waste, and are more than the people, who dwell on it, do, or can make use of, and so

still lie in common. Though this can scarce happen amongst that part of mankind that have consented to the use of money. . . .

Chapter IX. Of the Ends of Political Society and Government

If man in the state of nature be so free as has been said; if he be absolute lord of his own person and possessions, equal to the greatest, and subject to nobody, why will he part with his freedom, this empire, and subject himself to the dominion and control of any other power? To which 'tis obvious to answer, that though in the state of nature he has such a right, yet the enjoyment of it is very uncertain, and constantly exposed to the invasion of others; for all being kings as much as he, every man his equal, and the greater part no strict observers of equity and justice; the enjoyment of the property he has in this state is very unsafe, very insecure. This makes him willing to quit this condition, which however free, is full of fears and continual dangers: and 'tis not without reason, that he seeks out, and is willing to join in society with others who are already united, or have a mind to unite for the mutual preservation of their lives, liberties and estates, which I call by the general name, property.

124. The great and chief end therefore, of men uniting into commonwealths, and putting themselves under government, is the preservation of their property. To which in the state of nature there are many things wanting.

First, there wants an established, settled, known law, received and allowed by common consent to the standard of right and wrong, and the common measure to decide all controversies between them. For though the law of nature be plain and intelligible to all rational creatures; yet men being biased by their interest, as well as ignorant for want of study of it, are not apt to allow of it as a law binding them in the application of it to their particular cases.

125. Secondly, in the state of nature there wants a known and indifferent judge, with authority to determine all differences according to the established law. For every one in that state being both judge and executioner of the law of nature, men being partial to themselves, passion and revenge is very apt to carry them too far, and with too much heat in their own cases, as well as negligence and unconcernedness, make them too remiss in other men's.

126. Thirdly, in the state of nature there often wants power to back and support the sentence when right, and to give it due execution. They who by any injustice offended, will seldom fail, where they are

able, by force to make good their injustice; such resistance many times makes the punishment dangerous, and frequently destructive to those who attempt it.

127. Thus mankind, notwithstanding all the privileges of the state of nature, being but in an ill condition while they remain in it, are quickly driven into society. Hence it comes to pass, that we seldom find any number of men live any time together in this state. The inconveniencies that they are therein exposed to, by the irregular and uncertain exercise of the power every man has of punishing the transgressions of others, make them take sanctuary under the established laws of government, and therein seek the preservation of the property. 'Tis this makes them so willingly give up every one his single power of punishing to be exercised by such alone as shall be appointed to it amongst them; and by such rules as the community, or those authorized by them, to that purpose agree on. And in this we have the original right and rise of both the legislative and executive power, as well as of the governments and societies themselves. . . .

139. But government into whosesoever hands it is put, being as I have before shown, entrusted with this condition, and for this end, that men might have and secure their properties, the prince or senate, however it may have power to make laws for the regulating of property between the subjects one amongst another, yet can never have a power to take to themselves the whole, or any part of the subjects' property, without their own consent. For this would be in effect to leave them no property at all. And to let us see, that even absolute power, where it is necessary, is not arbitrary by being absolute, but is still limited by that reason, and confined to those ends which required it in some cases to be absolute, we need look no farther than the common practice of martial discipline. For the preservation of the army, and in it of the whole commonwealth, requires an absolute obedience to the command of every superior officer, and it is justly death to disobey or dispute the most dangerous or unreasonable of them; but yet we see, that neither the sergeant that could command a soldier to march up to the mouth of a cannon, or stand in a breach where he is almost sure to perish; can command that soldier to give him one penny of his money: nor the general that can condemn him to death for deserting his post, or not obeying the most desperate orders, cannot yet with all his absolute power of life and death, dispose of one farthing of that soldier's estate, or seize one jot of his goods; whom yet he can command any thing, and hang for the least disobedience. Because such a blind obedience is necessary to that end for which the

commander has his power, viz. the preservation of the rest, but the disposing of his goods has nothing to do with it.

140. 'Tis true, governments cannot be supported without great charge, and 'tis fit every one who enjoys his share of the protection, should pay, out of his estate, his proportion for the maintenance of it. But still it must be with his own consent, i.e., the consent of the majority, giving it either by themselves, or their representatives chosen by them; for if any one shall claim a power to lay and levy taxes on the people, by his own authority, and without such consent of the people, he thereby invades the fundamental law of property, and subverts the end of government. For what property have I in that which another may be right to take when he pleases to himself. . . .

158. *Salus Populi Suprema Lex,*[58] is certainly so just and fundamental a rule, that he who sincerely follows it cannot dangerously err. If therefore the executive, who has the power of convoking the legislative, observing rather the true proportion than fashion of representation, regulates not by old custom, but true reason, the number of members, in all places, that have a right to be distinctly represented, which no part of the people, however incorporated, can pretend to; but in proportion to the assistance which it affords to the public, it cannot be judged to have set up a new Legislative, but to have restored the old and true one, and to have rectified the disorders which succession of time had insensibly as well as inevitably introduced; for it being the interest as well as intention of the people to have a fair and equal representative; whoever brings it nearest to that, is an undoubted friend to, and establisher of the government, and cannot miss the consent and approbation of the community. Prerogative being nothing but a power in the hands of the prince to provide for the public good, in such cases, which depending upon unforeseen and uncertain occurrences, certain and unalterable laws could not safely direct. Whatsoever shall be done manifestly for the good of the people, and establishing the government upon its true foundations, is, and always will be, just prerogative. The power of erecting new corporations, and therewith new representatives, carries with it a supposition, that in time, the measures of representations might vary, and those have a just right to be represented which before had none; and by the same reason, those cease to have a right, and be too inconsiderable for such a privilege which before had it. 'Tis not a change from the present

[58]The welfare of the people is the highest law.

state which perhaps corruption or decay has introduced that makes an inroad upon the government, but the tendency of it to injure or oppress the people, and to set up one part or party with a distinction from, and an unequal subjection of the rest. Whatsoever cannot but be acknowledged to be of advantage to the society and people in general, upon just and lasting measures, will always, when done, justify itself; and whenever the people shall choose their representatives upon just and undeniably equal measures, suitable to the original frame of the government, it cannot be doubted to be the will and act of the society, whoever permitted or proposed to them so to do. . . .

203. May the commands then of a prince be opposed? May he be resisted, as often as any one shall find himself aggrieved, and but imagine he has not right done him? This will unhinge and overturn all polities, and, instead of government and order, leave nothing but anarchy and confusion.

204. To this I answer: that force is to be opposed to nothing but to unjust and unlawful force; whoever makes any opposition, in any other case, draws on himself a just condemnation, both from God and man; and so no such danger or confusion will follow, as is often suggested. . . .

Chapter XIX. Of the Dissolution of Governments

211. He that will, with any clearness, speak of the dissolution of government, ought, in the first place, to distinguish between the dissolution of the society, and the dissolution of the government. That which makes the community, and brings men out of the loose state of nature, into one politic society, is the agreement, which every one has, with the rest, to incorporate and act as one body, and so be one distinct commonwealth. . . .

212. Besides this overturning, from without, governments are dissolved from within: First, when the legislative is altered, civil society being a state of peace amongst those who are of it, from whom the state of war is excluded by the umpirage, which they have provided in their legislative, for the ending all difference, that may arise amongst any of them. 'Tis in their legislative, that the members of a commonwealth are united and combined together into one coherent, living body. This is the soul that gives form, life, and unity to the commonwealth: from hence the several members have their mutual influence, sympathy, and connection: and therefore, when the legislative is broken, or dissolved, dissolution and death follows. For the essence, and union of

the society consisting in having one will, the legislative, when once established by the majority, has the declaring, and, as it were, keeping of that will. The constitution of the legislative is the first and fundamental act of society, whereby provision is made for the continuation of their union, under the direction of persons, and bonds of laws, made by persons authorized thereunto, by the consent and appointment of the people, without which no one man, or number of men, amongst them, can have authority of making laws that shall be binding to the rest. When any one, or more, shall take upon them to make laws, whom the people have not appointed so to do, they make laws without authority, which the people are not therefore bound to obey; by which means they come again to be out of subjection, and may constitute to themselves a new legislative, as they think best, being in full liberty to resist the force of those, who, without authority, would impose any thing upon them. Every one is at the disposure of his own will, when those, who had, by the delegation of the society, the declaring of the public will, are excluded from it, and others usurp the place, who have no such authority or delegation.

213. This being usually brought about by such, in the commonwealth, who misuse the power they have: it is hard to consider it a right, and know at whose door to lay it, without knowing the form of government in which it happens. Let us suppose then the legislative placed in the concurrence of three distinct persons. First, a single, hereditary person having the constant, supreme, executive power, and, with it, the power of convoking, and dissolving the other two, within certain periods of time. Secondly, an assembly of hereditary nobility. Thirdly, an assembly of representatives chosen, *pro tempore*,[59] by the people: such a form of government supposed, it is evident:

214. First, that when such a single person, or prince sets up his own arbitrary will, in place of the laws, which are the will of the society, declared by the legislative, then the legislative is changed. For that being, in effect, the legislative whose rules and laws are put in execution, and required to be obeyed, when other laws are set up, and other rules pretended and enforced, than what the legislative, constituted by the society, have enacted, 'tis plain that the legislative is changed. Whoever introduced new laws, not being thereunto authorized by the fundamental appointment of the society, or subverts the old, disowns and overturns the power by which they were made, and so sets up a new legislative.

[59]For a time.

215. Secondly, when the prince hinders the legislative from assembling in its due time, or from acting freely, pursuant to those ends for which it was constituted, the legislative is altered. For 'tis not a certain number of men, no, nor their meeting, unless they have also freedom of debating, and leisure of perfecting what is for the good of the society, wherein the legislative consists, when these are taken away or altered so as to deprive the society of the due exercise of their power, the legislative is truly altered. For it is not names that constitute governments, but the use and exercise of those powers that were intended to accompany them: so that he who takes away the freedom, or hinders the acting of the legislative in due seasons, in effect takes away the legislative, and puts an end to the government.

216. Thirdly, when, by the arbitrary power of the prince, the electors, or ways of election are altered, without the consent, and contrary to the common interest of the people, there also the legislative is altered. For if others, than those whom the society hath authorized thereunto, do choose, or in another way than what the society hath prescribed, those chosen are not the legislative appointed by the people.

217. Fourthly, the delivery also of the people into the subjection of a foreign power, either by the prince, or by the legislative, is certainly a change of the legislative, and so a dissolution of the government. For the end, why people entered into society, being to be preserved one entire, free, independent society, to be governed by its own laws; this is lost whenever they are given up into the power of another. . . .

219. There is one way more, whereby such a government may be dissolved, and that is; when he, who has the supreme, executive power, neglects, and abandons that charge, so that the laws, already made, can no longer be put in execution. This is demonstratively to reduce all to anarchy, and so effectually to dissolve the government. For laws not being made for themselves, but to be by their execution the bonds of the society, to keep every part of the body politic in its due place and function, when that totally ceases, the government visibly ceases, the people become a confused multitude, without order or connection. Where there is no longer the administration of justice, for the securing of men's rights; nor any remaining power within the community to direct the force, or provide for the necessities of the public; there certainly is no government left. Where the laws cannot be executed it is all one as if there were no laws; and a government without laws, is I suppose, a mystery in politics, inconceivable to humane capacity, and inconsistent with humane society.

220. In these, and the like cases, when the government is dissolved, the people are at liberty to provide for themselves, by erecting a new legislative, differing from the other, by the change of persons, or form, or both, as they shall find it most for their safety and good. For the society can never, by the fault of another, lose the native and original right it has to preserve itself; which can only be done by a settled legislative, and a fair and impartial execution of the laws made by it. But the state of mankind is not so miserable, that they are not capable of using this remedy, 'till it be too late to look for any. To tell people they may provide for themselves, by erecting a new Legislative; when, by oppression, artifice, or being delivered over to a foreign power, their old one is gone, is only to tell them they may expect relief, when it is too late, and the evil is past cure. This is, in effect, no more than to bid them, first be slaves, and then to take care of their liberty; and, when their chains are on, tell them they may act like free men. This, if barely so, is rather mockery than relief, and men can never be secure from tyranny, if there be no means to escape it, 'till they are perfectly under it: and therefore it is, that they have not only a right to get out of it, but to prevent it. . . .

223. To this perhaps it will be said, that the people being ignorant and always discontented; to lay the foundation of government in the unsteady opinion and uncertain humor of the people, is to expose it to certain ruin: and no government will be able long to subsist, if the people may set up a new legislative whenever they take offence at the old one. To this I answer quite the contrary. People are not so easily got out of their old forms as some are apt to suggest. They are hardly to be prevailed with to amend the acknowledged faults in the frame they have been accustomed to. And if there be any original defects, or adventitious ones introduced by time or corruption; 'tis not an easy thing to get them changed, even when all the world sees there is an opportunity for it. This slowness and aversion in the people to quit their old constitutions, has in the many revolutions which have been seen in this kingdom, in this and former ages, still kept us to, or after some interval of fruitless attempts, still brought us back again to our old legislative of King, Lords and Commons: and whatever provocations have made the crown be taken from some of our Princes' heads, they never carried the people so far as to place it in another line.

224. But it will be said, this hypothesis lays a ferment for frequent rebellion. To which I answer:

First, no more than any other hypothesis. For when the people are made miserable, and find themselves exposed to the ill usage of arbitrary power; cry up their governors as much as you will for sons of Jupiter, let them be sacred and divine, descended or authorized from heaven; give them out for whom or what you please, the same will happen. The people generally ill-treated, and contrary to right, will be ready upon any occasion to ease themselves of a burden that sits heavy upon them. They will wish and seek for the opportunity, which in the change, weakness and accidents of human affairs seldom delays long to offer itself. He must have lived but a little while in the world, who has not seen examples of this in his time; and he must have read very little, who cannot produce examples of it in all sorts of governments in the world.

225. Secondly, I answer, such revolutions happen not upon every little mismanagement in public affairs. Great mistakes in the ruling part, many wrong and inconvenient laws, and all the slips of human frailty will be born by the people, without mutiny or murmur. But if a long train of abuses, prevarications and artifices, all tending the same way, make the design visible to the people, and they cannot but feel what they lie under, and see whither they are going; 'tis not to be wondered that they should then rouse themselves, and endeavor to put the rule into such hands which may secure to them the ends for which government was at first erected; and without which, ancient names and specious forms, are so far from being better, that they are much worse than the state of nature or pure anarchy; the inconveniencies being all as great and as near, but the remedy farther off and more difficult. . . .

229. The end of government is the good of mankind, and which is best for mankind, that the people should be always exposed to the boundless will of tyranny, or that the rulers should be sometimes liable to be opposed, when they grow exorbitant in the use of their power, and employ it for the destruction, and not the preservation of the properties of their people?

A Chronology of the Origins and Consequences of the Glorious Revolution (1649–1694)

1649 *January 30:* Execution of Charles I; England becomes a republic.

1660 *May 29:* Charles II restored as king of England, Scotland, and Ireland.

1662 *August 24:* Act of Uniformity goes into effect; non–Church of England clergymen leave their parishes.

1665–
1667 Second Anglo-Dutch War.

1666 *September:* Great Fire of London.

1672–
1674 Third Anglo-Dutch War.

1683 *June:* Rye House Plot to assassinate James and Charles II is revealed.

1685 *February 6:* Death of Charles II; accession of James II.

May 19: First meeting of James II's Parliament.

June 11: Duke of Monmouth lands in England, beginning rebellion.

July 5–6: Monmouth's rebellion crushed at Battle of Sedgemoor.

September: "Bloody Assizes"—the punishment of Monmouth's rebels.

October 8: Louis XIV revokes Edict of Nantes.

1686 *June:* Court discussion of war against Dutch.

1687 *April 4:* James II issues his first Declaration of Indulgence.

Autumn: James II's campaign to pack Parliament in order to repeal the Test Acts.

1688 *April 27:* James II issues his second Declaration of Indulgence.

June 29–30: Trial of seven Anglican bishops for refusing to read second Declaration of Indulgence.

June 30: Seven English noblemen invite Prince William of Orange to invade.

November 5: William lands at Torbay.

December 23: James II flees to France.

1689   *January 22–August 20:* First session of new Parliament; William and Mary are formally offered throne; Declaration of Rights is read.

April: Hearth tax is repealed.

May 7: England declares war on France.

May 24: Act of Toleration becomes law.

December: Land tax passes House of Commons.

1691   *April:* Low churchman John Tillotson becomes Archbishop of Canterbury.

1694   *May:* Bill establishing Bank of England passes.

Questions for Consideration

1. Do you agree that the Revolution of 1688–89 was a modern revolution? What do we mean by *revolution*? What distinguishes a revolution from a *coup d'état*? How does the Revolution of 1688–89 compare with other revolutions with which you are familiar, such as the French, Russian, American, or Mexican revolutions?

2. Why did James II abandon his country? Why do you think a king with a powerful army and a modern navy would flee his country without fighting?

3. Why did James II so dislike the Dutch? Why didn't he see Louis XIV's France as a threat to English interests? Why did William and Mary reverse his foreign policy?

4. We take religious toleration to be characteristic of a modern political life. Yet many in the seventeenth century argued passionately for intolerance. How did they justify their arguments?

5. John Locke advanced a powerful and influential argument for political resistance to tyrants. How did some seventeenth-century thinkers defend passive obedience? What arguments did they advance against political resistance?

6. How had English economy and society changed over the course of the seventeenth century?

7. Why do you think Richard Price and Edmund Burke were still debating the nature of the Revolution of 1688–89 in the late eighteenth century? Why did it still matter to them? Why might it matter to us?

8. How would you characterize the different approaches to the economy taken by the court of James II and that of William and Mary? Why do you think they thought differently?

9. The Revolution of 1688–89 was relatively bloodless. Do you think the lack of bloodshed was indicative of a lack of public political interest? Why or why not?

10. Would James II have been overthrown if he had not been a practicing Roman Catholic? Would a Protestant king pursuing the same policies have survived?

11. In October 1688, William offered his reasons for invading England. Compare these reasons with the Declaration of Rights (1689). Why do you think each document fails to include substantive discussions of political economy and foreign policy?

12. Were the changes that occurred in the immediate aftermath of the revolution the result of the actions of William III or the consequence of English popular sentiment?

Selected Bibliography

The Revolution of 1688–89 has attracted little scholarship compared to other revolutions. The best recent work remains in article form. Nevertheless, the student interested in the period can learn a great deal from earlier monographs and collections as well.

ON REVOLUTIONS IN GENERAL

Arendt, Hannah. *On Revolution*. London: Penguin, 1963. The philosopher discusses the meaning of revolution, focusing heavily on the French and American revolutions as contrasting cases.

Dunn, John. *Modern Revolutions*. Cambridge: Cambridge University Press, 1972. Dunn compares a number of twentieth-century revolutions in his effort to define the nature of modern revolutions. It is worth considering his definition in light of this discussion of the Revolution of 1688–89.

Skocpol, Theda. *States and Social Revolutions*. Cambridge: Cambridge University Press, 1979. This is a seminal text in the comparative study of revolutions.

ON THE REVOLUTION OF 1688–1689

Israel, Jonathan. *The Anglo-Dutch Moment: Essays on the Glorious Revolution and Its World Impact*. Cambridge: Cambridge University Press, 1991. This is the best collection of essays commemorating the 300th anniversary of the revolution. It is especially strong on William's preparations for the invasion, the European context, and political thought in the 1690s.

Jones, J. R. *The Revolution of 1688 in England*. New York: W. W. Norton, 1972. This book takes James II's aspirations seriously and offers a compelling description of the European geopolitical scene.

Macaulay, Thomas Babington. *History of England from the Accession of James II*. New York: Dutton, 1910. This was for a long time the standard account of the revolution. It remains an admirable piece of scholarship.

Speck, W. A. *Reluctant Revolutionaries: Englishmen and the Revolution of 1688*. Oxford: Oxford University Press, 1988. This is the most recent scholarly monograph on the revolution.

Trevelyan, G. M. *The English Revolution, 1688–89*. Oxford: Oxford University Press, 1965. In delightful prose, Trevelyan updates the argument presented by Macaulay.

Webb, Stephen Saunders. *Lord Churchill's Coup*. New York: Alfred A. Knopf, 1995. This book is very good on the military and colonial dimensions of the revolution.

ENGLAND'S ECONOMY

Clay, C. G. A. *Economic Expansion and Social Change: England, 1500–1700*. Cambridge: Cambridge University Press, 1984. This is the most comprehensive survey of social and economic change in Early Modern England.

Coleman, D. C. *The Economy of England, 1450–1750*. Oxford: Oxford University Press, 1977. This is still the best introduction to the Early Modern English economy.

THE REVOLUTIONARY MOMENT

Beddard, Robert. "The Unexpected Whig Revolution of 1688." In Beddard, ed., *The Revolutions of 1688*. Oxford: Clarendon Press, 1991, 11–101. This, together with Miller's "Proto-Jacobinism?" essay, demonstrates that the old story of English political consensus during the autumn and winter of 1688–89 covers up more than it clarifies.

Harris, Tim. "Reluctant Revolutionaries? The Scots and the Revolution of 1688–89." In Howard Nenner, ed., *Politics and the Political Imagination in Later Stuart Britain*. Rochester: University of Rochester Press, 1997, 97–117. This essay attempts to assess the significance of the Revolution of 1688-89 in England by contrasting it with events in Scotland. The comparison of events in London and Edinburgh prompts curiosity about the nature of events outside the capitals in these crucial months.

Miller, John. "Proto-Jacobitism? The Tories and the Revolution of 1688–89." In Eveline Cruickshanks and Jeremy Black, eds., *The Jacobite Challenge*. Edinburgh: John Donald, 1988, 7–23. This essay chronicles Tory support and aspirations in late 1688–89.

CONSTITUTIONAL CHANGE

Goldie, Mark. "The Revolution of 1689 and the Structure of Political Argument," *Bulletin of Research in the Humanities* 83 (1980): 473–564. This carefully researched essay demonstrates the range of arguments used to defend the constitutional settlement of 1689.

Kenyon, J. P. *Revolution Principles: The Politics of Party, 1689–1720*. Cambridge: Cambridge University Press, 1977. This work was one of the first systematic studies of political thought after the revolution. It argues for greater continuity from the period before the revolution than is suggested here.

Schwoerer, Lois. *The Declaration of Rights, 1689*. Baltimore: Johns Hopkins University Press, 1981. This book remains the best study of this important document.

FOREIGN POLICY

Baxter, Stephen. *William III and the Defense of European Liberty, 1650–1702*. New York: Harcourt, Brace and World, 1966. Little attention has been paid to James II's foreign policy, but this biography does a good job of detailing William's European interests.

POLITICAL ECONOMY

Appleby, Joyce. *Economic Thought and Ideology in Seventeenth Century England*. Princeton: Princeton University Press, 1978. Little attention has been paid to the political economy of James II, but this is an admirable survey of economic writing in the seventeenth century. It is very much an intellectual history.

Brewer, John. *The Sinews of Power: War, Money and the English State, 1688–1783*. New York: Alfred A. Knopf, 1988. This book is the best discussion of the revolutionary transformation of the English state after 1689.

Dickson, P. G. M. *The Financial Revolution in England*. London: St. Martin's, 1967. A useful study of the transformation of England's financial machinery after the Revolution.

CHURCH OF ENGLAND

Spurr, John. *The Restoration Church of England, 1646–1689*. New Haven: Yale University Press, 1991. This work contains the best discussion of the theology and practice of the Church of England in the late seventeenth century.

Index

177

Dominion of the West Indies, 23
Dutch East India Company, 19
Dutch Republic
    alliance with, 97
    Anglo-Dutch wars, 85*n*, 86, 89*n*, 91, 95
    anti-Dutch policy, 82–86, 91–94, 98–99
    Carthage comparison, 85*n*
    exiles in, 18
    fear of France and, 89–90
    fishing industry, 23–24
    Franco-Dutch War, 89*n*
    freedoms in, 92–93
    imperial policy, 23
    invasion attempt, 1
    manufacturing, 8
    military power of, 19
    as model for England, 32
    religious practices in, 19, 92, 93
    Revolution of 1688–89 and, 33
    taxation in, 92–93
    as threat to England, 18–20, 21, 22, 82–86, 95
    trade, 19, 91–92, 108–11

"Early Defense of the Bank of England, An," 115–19
East India Company, 3, 22, 23, 24, 25, 63–64, 102, 107, 122
    Land Bank and, 115
    limits on, 25
    role of, 109–11
    trade principles and, 103–7
East India Company v. Sandys, 103–7
East Indies, 23
    Dutch Republic trade with, 91
    trade with, 32, 63, 109–11, 113–14
Ecclesiastical Commission, 14, 71
"Economies of Fisheries, The" (L'Estrange), 145–47
economy. *See also* political economy; trade
    Dutch Republic, 8
    England, 7–11
Edict of Nantes, 21
"Effects of the New Long-Distance Trades, The," 64–66
Elizabeth, Queen, 1, 2, 63
England
    alliance with Dutch Republic, 97
    anti-Dutch policy, 82–86, 98–99
    anti-French policy, 82, 95–102
    armies, 12, 14, 22, 32, 38
    balance of trade with France, 100
    bureaucracy, 32
    civil wars, 10, 11, 17, 55
    coffeehouses, 66–68
    Constitution, 15–17

diet, 61–62
Dutch Republic as threat to, 18–20, 21, 86
economy, 7–11, 55
failed invasions of, 1–2
fishing industry, 23–24, 145–47
foreign policy, 17–21, 82–102
France as threat to, 20–21, 24, 123
fuels, 61
geopolitics, 120–21
housing, 57–61
imperial policy, 23
manufacturing, 22, 32, 112–13
modernization of, 11, 14, 15, 31–32
navy, 12, 14, 22
political economy, 21–26, 102–23, 158–67
politics, 11–17
population policy, 114–15
self-defense of, 120
social issues, 55–68
social life, 57–64
standing army, 70, 87
trade, 10–11, 55–56, 63–66, 91–92, 107–15, 120–23
trade with East Indies, 32, 63, 109–11, 113–14
trade with France, 20
travel, 62–63
urbanization of, 8–9
warfare, 22
war with France, 3, 21, 31, 98–102, 170
wealth of, 112–13
William of Orange invited to, 1–2, 37–39
William's reasons for invading, 2, 39–43
Enlightenment, 31*n*
"Establishing Principles of Trade in *East India Company v. Sandys*," 103–7
Evelyn, John, "Diary Entries concerning France," 94–95
Evelyn, John, Jr., 95
Exclusion Campaign, 93*n*

Fagel, Gaspar, 38, 137
Fifth Monarchy Men, 26
fines, 70
firefighters, 59–60
fishing industry, 23–24, 32, 145–47
Fitzroy, Henry. *See* Grafton, Duke of
foreign policy, 17–21, 82–102. *See also* Dutch Republic; France
    James II's memoirs on, 87–91
    Revolution of 1688–89 and, 82, 87–91